The New Temple Shakespeare

Edited by M. R. RIDLEY, M.A.

KING HENRY IV
FIRST PART

by William Shakespeare

J. M. DENT & SONS LTD., London
E. P. DUTTON & CO., INC., New York

Decorated by Eric Gill

First published in 1935

Published in this edition
by arrangement with E. P. Dutton & Co., Inc.,
201 Park Avenue South, New York, N.Y. 10003
and J. M. Dent & Sons Ltd.,
Bedford Street, London.

PRINTED IN THE UNITED STATES OF AMERICA

Editor's General Note

THE TEXT. The editor has kept before him the aim of presenting to the modern reader the nearest possible approximation to what Shakespeare actually wrote. The text is therefore conservative, and is based on the earliest reliable printed text. But to avoid distraction (*a*) the spelling is modernised, and (*b*) a limited number of universally accepted emendations is admitted without comment. Where a Quarto text exists as well as the First Folio the passages which occur only in the Quarto are enclosed in square brackets [ ] and those which occur only in the Folio in brace brackets { }.

SCENE DIVISION. The rapid continuity of the Elizabethan curtainless production is lost by the 'traditional' scene divisions. Where there is an essential difference of place these scene divisions are retained. Where on the other hand the change of place is insignificant the scene division is indicated only by a space on the page. For ease of reference, however, the 'traditional' division is retained at the head of the page and in line numbering.

NOTES. Passages on which there are notes are indicated by a † in the margin.

PUNCTUATION adheres more closely than has been usual to the 'Elizabethan' punctuation of the early texts. It is often therefore more indicative of the way in which the lines were to be delivered than of their syntactical construction.

GLOSSARIES are arranged on a somewhat novel principle, not alphabetically, but in the order in which the words or phrases occur. The editor is much indebted to Mr. J. N. Bryson for his collaboration in the preparation of the glossaries.

Preface

THE TEXT. The First Quarto was published in 1598 with the following title-page: THE / HISTORY OF / HENRIE THE / FOURTH; / With the battell at Shrewsburie, / *betweene the King and Lord* / Henry Percy, surnamed / Henrie Hotspur of / the North. / *With the humorous conceits of Sir* / Iohn Falstalffe. / AT LONDON, / Printed by *P. S.* for *Andrew Wise*, dwelling / in Paules Churchyard, at the signe of / the Angell. 1598. /

In the course of the next fifteen years four more quartos appeared. These, in spite of all announcing themselves as 'newly corrected by W. Shakespeare,' in fact show a steady accumulation of errors, Q 5 being unhappily the worst offender. As illustrating what was liable to happen to a text in the course of transmission it is perhaps worth while to give some notion of this cumulative process. Of fifty instances of variant reading in Act V. Q 1, apart from 3 misspellings, seems to be 'wrong' in 5 instances, 'doubtful' in 4, and 'right' in the remaining 38. Q 2 makes 2 corrections, attempts 1 emendation, and introduces 7 new errors of its own. Q 3 copies these 7 and introduces 1 more. Q 4 copies these 8 and introduces 4 more. Q 5 makes 3 corrections, and attempts 1 emendation, but also introduces 12 new errors. The Folio text was based on Q 5, perhaps on a copy which had to some extent, though most imperfectly, been corrected by Q 1. Taking these same instances, F 1 makes 13 corrections, of which 9 are reversions to Q 1 and the other 4 are its own. On the other hand it accepts 13 errors of Q 5 which reference to Q 1 would have corrected, and also introduces 7 new ones of its own. And study of the other acts shows the same process at work, each successive Quarto increasing on balance the number of errors, the Folio making some attempt to diminish their number, but introducing some new ones of its own. One or two well known and significant instances may be given in detail.

In V. iii. 11 Q 1 reads:

I was not borne a yeelder thou proud Scot,

This, with the addition of a comma between *yeelder* and *thou,* is maintained up till Q 4. The peccant Q 5 then produces:

I was not borne to yield, thou proud Scot,

The editor or compositor of F finding this unmetrical line before him decides that something must be done about it, and emends to:

I was not borne to yeeld, thou haughty Scot,

Again, in V. iv. 84, Q 1 reads:

But that the earthy and cold hand of death

Here Q 2 is the sinner and reads:

But that the earth and cold hand of death

and this is maintained up till Q 5. Again F makes the line scan:

But that the Earth, and the cold hand of death,

In both cases, that is, F produces a perfectly good line; the first in the absence of the Quarto would have been entirely above suspicion, even if the second had been felt to be slightly awkward; but neither line, we may be almost certain, is what Shakespeare wrote.

Apart from these various isolated verbal differences there is one general difference between the Quarto and Folio texts. The latter has suffered from, or at any rate has experienced, that process of expurgation or deprofanisation which the Folio always exhibits, but which has here been carried out with most uncommon completeness and rigour. It has been suggested that the Folio may have been printed from a copy of Q 5 which had been revised with a view to a performance at Court, where, presumably, it was good policy to pay exact attention to the 'Act to Restrain the Abuses of Players.' At any rate, whatever the reason, 'God' throughout becomes 'heaven,' ''Zounds' and ''Sblood' fade into 'in faith,' and 'in faith' for the most part disappears altogether; the poor reviser disentangles himself as best he can from the resultant difficulties, and Hotspur's speech to his wife on swearing takes on a new irony.

The text here given adheres throughout as closely as possible to Q 1, except in the matter of line-division. The play is full of passages which seem to be anything from 'almost' to 'half-way-towards' verse, and Q is inconsistent in its treatment. There are no omissions by either text of passages which occur in the other, and it would be merely vexatious to indicate the continual omission of oaths by the Folio.

DATE OF COMPOSITION. The *terminus ad quem* is February 1598, when the play was entered in the Stationers' Registers. The *terminus a quo* is uncertain. There can be no reasonable doubt that when the play first appeared Falstaff was Oldcastle (the tradition, dating from about 1625, is supported by various signs in the text, notably the allusion in I. ii. 41, the metrical need for a trisyllable in II. ii. 103, and the apology in the Epilogue to Part II). But I can see no reason to suppose that this implies an interval of 'many months' between the first performance and the publication of the play. All that is needed is time for a few performances at which offence was taken by the descendants of Sir John Oldcastle, Lord Cobham, the famous Lollard who was martyred in 1418, and time for Shakespeare to remove the cause of offence by an alteration of name throughout. If we put the composition of the play in 1597 we shall not be far wrong.

SOURCES. The main source of the play is Holinshed's *Chronicles*. But Shakespeare, as usual, modifies Holinshed to suit his dramatic purposes. In particular he plays fast and loose with the ages of his characters. Henry IV, represented throughout the play as at least middle-aged, was, in fact, in his thirties, and younger than Hotspur, who has to be rejuvenated to act as a foil to Prince Hal. The projected crusade is antedated by some ten years, and the interview between the Prince and his father by several.

For the historical part of the play Shakespeare may also have been indebted to Daniel's *History of the Civil Wars* (1595) and to the ballad of *Chevy Chase.*

For the Falstaff sections of the play Shakespeare was in some measure indebted to a play produced about 1588 called *The Famous Victories of Henry V.* In this, apart from the caricature of Sir John Oldcastle, there is the picture of the riotous young prince and his disreputable companions frequenting the 'old tavern in Eastcheap' and conducting a highway robbery. There is also an interview between the Prince and the King, and a scene which seems to be at least a foreshadowing of the scene in the tavern in which the Prince and Falstaff in turn play the King. And there are various other minor similarities. But the essential debt is of the slightest.

DURATION OF ACTION. The historical time covered is from June 22, 1402 (Mortimer's defeat by Glendower), to July 21, 1403 (the battle of Shrewsbury). Daniel computes the dramatic time at three months or thereabouts, with ten 'historic' days, and three extra or Falstaffian days. The main intervals on this scheme are a week after I. i., three or four weeks after I. iii., a week after II. iii., and a fortnight after III. i.

CRITICISM. Since the critics usually consider together the two parts of *Henry IV*, if not the whole "great national trilogy which is at once the flower of Shakespeare's second period and the crown of his achievements in historic drama," it will be more satisfactory to give some extracts from them in Part II. It is perhaps here enough to suggest the importance of reading the two parts not as two independent though connected plays, but as parts of one whole. Unless we do so we are apt to miss the steady development of the two main characters, upwards in the one case and downwards in the other, and the relation between the two developments, which prepare us for the figure of Henry V and for the Rejection of Falstaff.

KING HENRY IV
PART I

DRAMATIS PERSONÆ

KING HENRY *the Fourth.*
HENRY, *Prince of Wales,*
JOHN *of Lancaster,* } *sons to the King.*
EARL OF WESTMORELAND.
SIR WALTER BLUNT.
THOMAS PERCY, *Earl of Worcester.*
HENRY PERCY, *Earl of Northumberland.*
HENRY PERCY, *surnamed* HOTSPUR, *his son.*
EDMUND MORTIMER, *Earl of March.*
RICHARD SCROOP, *Archbishop of York.*
ARCHIBALD, *Earl of Douglas.*
OWEN GLENDOWER.
SIR RICHARD VERNON.
SIR JOHN FALSTAFF.
SIR MICHAEL, *a friend to the Archbishop of York.*
POINS.
GADSHILL.
PETO.
BARDOLPH.
FRANCIS, *a drawer.*

LADY PERCY, *wife to Hotspur, and sister to Mortimer.*
LADY MORTIMER, *daughter to Glendower, and wife to Mortimer.*
MISTRESS QUICKLY, *hostess of a tavern in Eastcheap.*

Lords, Officers, Sheriff, Vintner, Chamberlain, Drawers, two Carriers, Travellers, and Attendants.

SCENE: *England.*

THE FIRST PART OF
KING HENRY IV

Act First

SCENE I

London. The palace

*Enter King Henry, Lord John of Lancaster, the Earl of West-
moreland, Sir Walter Blunt, and others*

King. So shaken as we are, so wan with care,
    Find we a time for frighted peace to pant,
    And breathe short-winded accents of new broils
    To be commenc'd in stronds afar remote.
    No more the thirsty entrance of this soil   †
    Shall daub her lips with her own children's blood,
    No more shall trenching war channel her fields,
    Nor bruise her flowerets with the armed hoofs
    Of hostile paces: those opposed eyes,
    Which, like the meteors of a troubled heaven,   10
    All of one nature, of one substance bred,
    Did lately meet in the intestine shock
    And furious close of civil butchery,
    Shall now, in mutual well-beseeming ranks,
    March all one way, and be no more oppos'd
    Against acquaintance, kindred and allies:
    The edge of war, like an ill-sheathed knife,
    No more shall cut his master: therefore, friends,
    As far as to the sepulchre of Christ,
    Whose soldier now, under whose blessed cross   20
    We are impressed and engag'd to fight,

Forthwith a power of English shall we levy,
Whose arms were moulded in their mothers' womb
To chase these pagans in those holy fields,
Over whose acres walk'd those blessed feet,
Which fourteen hundred years ago were nail'd,
For our advantage, on the bitter cross.
But this our purpose now is twelve month old,
And bootless 'tis to tell you we will go:
Therefore we meet not now: then let me hear   †
Of you, my gentle cousin Westmoreland,   31
What yesternight our council did decree
In forwarding this dear expedience.
Westmoreland. My liege, this haste was hot in question,
And many limits of the charge set down
But yesternight, when all athwart there came
A post from Wales, loaden with heavy news,
Whose worst was that the noble Mortimer,
Leading the men of Herefordshire to fight
Against the irregular and wild Glendower,   40
Was by the rude hands of that Welshman taken,
A thousand of his people butchered;
Upon whose dead corpse there was such misuse,
Such beastly shameless transformation,
By those Welshwomen done, as may not be,
Without much shame, retold, or spoken of.
King. It seems then that the tidings of this broil
Brake off our business for the Holy Land.
Westmoreland. This match'd with other did, my gracious
    lord;
For more uneven and unwelcome news   50
Came from the north, and thus it did import;
On Holy-rood day, the gallant Hotspur there,
Young Harry Percy, and brave Archibald,
That ever-valiant and approved Scot,
At Holmedon met,
Where they did spend a sad and bloody hour;
As by discharge of their artillery,

2

And shape of likelihood, the news was told;
For he that brought them, in the very heat
And pride of their contention did take horse,   60
Uncertain of the issue any way.
King. Here is a dear, a true industrious friend,
Sir Walter Blunt, new lighted from his horse,
Stain'd with the variation of each soil
Betwixt that Holmedon and this seat of ours;
And he hath brought us smooth and welcome news,
The Earl of Douglas is discomfited,
Ten thousand bold Scots, two and twenty knights,
Balk'd in their own blood did Sir Walter see
On Holmedon's plains, of prisoners, Hotspur took   70
Mordake Earl of Fife, and eldest son
To beaten Douglas, and the Earl of Athol,
Of Murray, Angus, and Menteith:
And is not this an honourable spoil?
A gallant prize? ha, cousin, is it not?
Westmoreland. In faith it is.
A conquest for a prince to boast of.
King. Yea, there thou mak'st me sad and mak'st me sin
In envy, that my Lord Northumberland
Should be the father to so blest a son: 80
A son who is the theme of honour's tongue,
Amongst a grove, the very straightest plant,
Who is sweet Fortune's minion and her pride,
Whilst I by looking on the praise of him
See riot and dishonour stain the brow
Of my young Harry. O that it could be prov'd
That some night-tripping fairy had exchang'd
In cradle-clothes our children where they lay,
And call'd mine Percy, his Plantagenet,
Then would I have his Harry, and he mine!   90
But let him from my thoughts. What think you, coz,
Of this young Percy's pride? the prisoners,
Which he in this adventure hath surpris'd,
To his own use he keeps, and sends me word

3

I shall have none but Mordake Earl of Fife.
Westmoreland. This is his uncle's teaching: this is
    Worcester,
Malevolent to you in all aspects,
Which makes him prune himself, and bristle up
The crest of youth against your dignity.
King. But I have sent for him to answer this;   100
And for this cause awhile we must neglect
Our holy purpose to Jerusalem.
Cousin, on Wednesday next our council we
Will hold at Windsor; so inform the lords:
But come yourself with speed to us again,
For more is to be said and to be done
Than out of anger can be uttered.
Westmoreland. I will, my liege.   *Exeunt*

SCENE II

London. An apartment of the Prince's

Enter the Prince of Wales and Falstaff

Falstaff. Now, Hal, what time of day is it, lad?
Prince. Thou art so fat-witted, with drinking of old sack,
    and unbuttoning thee after supper, and sleeping upon
    benches after noon, that thou hast forgotten to de-
    mand that truly which thou wouldst truly know. What
    a devil hast thou to do with the time of the day? Un-
    less hours were cups of sack, and minutes capons, and
    clocks the tongues of bawds, and dials the signs of
    leaping-houses, and the blessed sun himself a fair hot
    wench in flame-coloured taffeta, I see no reason why   10
    thou shouldst be so superfluous to demand the time of
    the day.
Falstaff. Indeed, you come near me now, Hal, for we that
    take purses go by the moon and the seven stars, and
    not by Phœbus, he, 'that wandering knight so fair.'
    And, I prithee, sweet wag, when thou art king, as, God

4

save thy grace,—majesty I should say, for grace thou
wilt have none,—

Prince. What, none?

Falstaff. No, by my troth, not so much as will serve to be   20
prologue to an egg and butter.

Prince. Well, how then? come, roundly, roundly.

Falstaff. Marry, then, sweet wag, when thou art king, let
not us that are squires of the night's body be called
thieves of the day's beauty: let us be Diana's foresters,
gentlemen of the shade, minions of the moon, and let
men say we be men of good government, being governed as the sea is, by our noble and chaste mistress
the moon, under whose countenance we steal.

Prince. Thou sayest well, and it holds well too, for the   30
fortune of us that are the moon's men doth ebb and
flow like the sea, being governed as the sea is by the
moon. As, for proof, now: a purse of gold most reso-
lutely snatch'd on Monday night and most dissolutely
spent on Tuesday morning, got with swearing 'Lay by'
and spent with crying 'Bring in,' now in as low an ebb
as the foot of the ladder, and by and by in as high a
flow as the ridge of the gallows.

Falstaff. By the Lord, thou say'st true, lad, and is not my
hostess of the tavern a most sweet wench?   40

Prince. As the honey of Hybla, my old lad of the castle,
and is not a buff jerkin a most sweet robe of durance?

Falstaff. How now, how now, mad wag? what, in thy
quips and thy quiddities? what a plague have I to do
with a buff jerkin?

Prince. Why, what a pox have I to do with my hostess of
the tavern?

Falstaff. Well, thou hast call'd her to a reckoning many a
time and oft.

Prince. Did I ever call for thee to pay thy part?   50

Falstaff. No; I'll give thee thy due, thou hast paid all
there.

Prince. Yea, and elsewhere, so far as my coin would

5

stretch, and where it would not, I have used my credit.

Falstaff. Yea, and so us'd it that, were it not here apparent that thou art heir apparent—But, I prithee, sweet wag, shall there be gallows standing in England when thou art king? and resolution thus fobb'd as it is with the rusty curb of old father antic the law? Do not thou, when thou art king, hang a thief.   60

Prince. No, thou shalt.

Falstaff. Shall I? O rare! By the Lord, I'll be a brave judge.

Prince. Thou judgest false already; I mean, thou shalt have the hanging of the thieves, and so become a rare hangman.

Falstaff. Well, Hal, well, and in some sort it jumps with my humour, as well as waiting in the court, I can tell you.

Prince. For obtaining of suits?   70

Falstaff. Yea, for obtaining of suits, whereof the hangman hath no lean wardrobe. 'Sblood, I am as melancholy as a gib cat, or a lugg'd bear.

Prince. Or an old lion, or a lover's lute.

Falstaff. Yea, or the drone of a Lincolnshire bagpipe.

Prince. What sayest thou to a hare, or the melancholy of Moor-ditch?

Falstaff. Thou hast the most unsavoury similes, and art indeed the most comparative rascalliest sweet young prince. But, Hal, I prithee trouble me no more with   80 vanity; I would to God thou and I knew where a commodity of good names were to be bought. An old lord of the council rated me the other day in the street about you, sir, but I mark'd him not, and yet he talk'd very wisely, but I regarded him not, and yet he talk'd wisely, and in the street too.

Prince. Thou didst well, for [wisdom cries out in the streets and] no man regards it.

Falstaff. O, thou hast damnable iteration, and art indeed able to corrupt a saint: thou hast done much harm   90

6

upon me, Hal, God forgive thee for it! Before I knew thee, Hal, I knew nothing, and now am I, if a man should speak truly, little better than one of the wicked: I must give over this life, and I will give it over: by the Lord, an I do not, I am a villain; I'll be damn'd for never a king's son in Christendom.

Prince. Where shall we take a purse to-morrow, Jack?

Falstaff. 'Zounds, where thou wilt, lad, I'll make one; an I do not, call me villain and baffle me.

Prince. I see a good amendment of life in thee, from   100 praying to purse-taking.

Falstaff. Why, Hal, 'tis my vocation, Hal, 'tis no sin for a man to labour in his vocation.

Enter Poins

Poins! Now shall we know if Gadshill have set a match. O, if men were to be sav'd by merit, what hole in hell were hot enough for him? This is the most omnipotent villain that ever cried 'Stand' to a true man.

Prince. Good morrow, Ned.

Poins. Good morrow, sweet Hal. What says Monsieur Remorse? what says Sir John Sack, and Sugar Jack?   †   how agrees the devil and thee about thy soul, that thou   111 soldest him on Good Friday last, for a cup of Madeira and a cold capon's leg?

Prince. Sir John stands to his word, the devil shall have his bargain, for he was never yet a breaker of proverbs: he will give the devil his due.

Poins. Then art thou damn'd for keeping thy word with the devil.

Prince. Else he had been damn'd for cozening the devil.

Poins. But, my lads, my lads, to-morrow morning, by four   120 o'clock early at Gadshill, there are pilgrims going to Canterbury with rich offerings, and traders riding to London with fat purses. I have vizards for you all, you have horses for yourselves, Gadshill lies to-night in Rochester, I have bespoke supper to-morrow night in

Eastcheap: we may do it as secure as sleep; if you will
go, I will stuff your purses full of crowns; if you will
not, tarry at home and be hang'd.

Falstaff. Hear ye, Yedward, if I tarry at home and go not,
I'll hang you for going.   130

Poins. You will, chops?

Falstaff. Hal, wilt thou make one?

Prince. Who, I rob? I a thief? not I, by my faith.

Falstaff. There's neither honesty, manhood, nor good fellowship in thee, nor thou cam'st not of the blood royal,
if thou darest not stand for ten shillings.

Prince. Well then, once in my days I'll be a madcap.

Falstaff. Why, that's well said.

Prince. Well, come what will, I'll tarry at home.

Falstaff. By the Lord, I'll be a traitor then, when thou art   140
king.

Prince. I care not.

Poins. Sir John, I prithee leave the prince and me alone; I
will lay him down such reasons for this adventure that
he shall go.

Falstaff. Well, God give thee the spirit of persuasion, and
him the ears of profiting, that what thou speakest, may
move, and what he hears, may be believed, that the
true prince may (for recreation sake) prove a false
thief, for the poor abuses of the time want counte-   150
nance: farewell, you shall find me in Eastcheap.

Prince. Farewell, the latter spring! farewell, All-hallown
summer!   *Exit Falstaff*

Poins. Now, my good sweet honey lord, ride with us to-
morrow. I have a jest to execute, that I cannot manage
alone. Falstaff, Bardolph, Peto and Gadshill shall rob
those men that we have already waylaid, yourself and
I will not be there; and when they have the booty, if
you and I do not rob them, cut this head off from my
shoulders.   160

Prince. How shall we part with them in setting forth?

Poins. Why, we will set forth before or after them, and

appoint them a place of meeting, wherein it is at our
pleasure to fail; and then will they adventure upon the
exploit themselves, which they shall have no sooner
achiev'd but we'll set upon them.

Prince. Yea, but 'tis like that they will know us by our
horses, by our habits, and by every other appointment,
to be ourselves.

Poins. Tut! our horses they shall not see, I'll tie them in   170
the wood; our vizards we will change after we leave
them: and, sirrah, I have cases of buckram for the
nonce, to immask our noted outward garments.

Prince. Yea, but I doubt they will be too hard for us.

Poins. Well, for two of them, I know them to be as true-
bred cowards as ever turn'd back; and for the third, if
he fight longer than he sees reason, I'll forswear arms.
The virtue of this jest will be the incomprehensible lies
that this same fat rogue will tell us when we meet at
supper, how thirty at least he fought with, what wards,   180
what blows, what extremities he endured; and in the
reproof of this lives the jest.

Prince. Well, I'll go with thee: provide us all things nec-
essary, and meet me to-morrow night in Eastcheap;
there I'll sup. Farewell.

Poins. Farewell, my lord.   *Exit*

Prince. I know you all, and will a while uphold
The unyok'd humour of your idleness;
Yet herein will I imitate the sun,
Who doth permit the base contagious clouds   190
To smother up his beauty from the world,
That, when he please again to be himself,
Being wanted, he may be more wonder'd at
By breaking through the foul and ugly mists
Of vapours that did seem to strangle him.
If all the year were playing holidays,
To sport would be as tedious as to work;
But when they seldom come, they wish'd for come,
And nothing pleaseth but rare accidents.

9

So, when this loose behaviour I throw off,   200
And pay the debt I never promised,
By how much better than my word I am,
By so much shall I falsify men's hopes,
And like bright metal on a sullen ground,
My reformation, glittering o'er my fault,
Shall show more goodly, and attract more eyes,
Than that which hath no foil to set it off.
I'll so offend, to make offence a skill;
Redeeming time when men think least I will.   *Exit*

SCENE III

London. The palace

Enter the King, Northumberland, Worcester, Hotspur, Sir Walter Blunt, with others

King. My blood hath been too cold and temperate,
Unapt to stir at these indignities,
And you have found me; for accordingly
You tread upon my patience: but be sure
I will from henceforth rather be myself,
Mighty, and to be fear'd, than my condition,   †
Which hath been smooth as oil, soft as young down,
And therefore lost that title of respect
Which the proud soul ne'er pays but to the proud.
Worcester. Our house, my sovereign liege, little deserves   10
The scourge of greatness to be us'd on it,
And that same greatness too, which our own hands
Have holp to make so portly.
Northumberland. My lord,—
King. Worcester, get thee gone, for I do see
Danger and disobedience in thine eye:
O, sir, your presence is too bold and peremptory,
And majesty might never yet endure
The moody frontier of a servant brow.
You have good leave to leave us: when we need   20

Your use and counsel, we shall send for you.
                                    Exit Worcester
(*to Northumberland*) You were about to speak.
Northumberland.   Yea, my good lord.
  Those prisoners in your highness' name demanded,
  Which Harry Percy here at Holmedon took,
  Were, as he says, not with such strength denied
  As is delivered to your majesty:
  Either envy, therefore, or misprision,
  Is guilty of this fault, and not my son.
Hotspur. My liege, I did deny no prisoners;
  But I remember when the fight was done,   30
  When I was dry with rage, and extreme toil,
  Breathless and faint, leaning upon my sword,
  Came there a certain lord, neat and trimly dress'd,
  Fresh as a bridegroom, and his chin new reap'd
  Show'd like a stubble-land at harvest-home;
  He was perfumed like a milliner,
  And 'twixt his finger and his thumb he held
  A pouncet-box, which ever and anon
  He gave his nose, and took 't away again,
  Who therewith angry, when it next came there,   40
  Took it in snuff, and still he smil'd and talk'd:
  And as the soldiers bore dead bodies by,
  He call'd them untaught knaves, unmannerly,
  To bring a slovenly unhandsome corse
  Betwixt the wind and his nobility:
  With many holiday and lady terms
  He question'd me; amongst the rest, demanded
  My prisoners in your majesty's behalf.
  I then, all smarting with my wounds being cold,
  To be so pester'd with a popinjay,   50
  Out of my grief and my impatience
  Answer'd neglectingly, I know not what,
  He should, or he should not; for he made me mad
  To see him shine so brisk, and smell so sweet,
  And talk so like a waiting-gentlewoman,

11

Of guns, and drums, and wounds,—God save the
    mark!—
And telling me the sovereign'st thing on earth
Was parmaceti for an inward bruise,
And that it was great pity, so it was,
This villanous salt-petre should be digg'd   60
Out of the bowels of the harmless earth,
Which many a good tall fellow had destroy'd
So cowardly, and but for these vile guns
He would himself have been a soldier.
This bald unjointed chat of his, my lord,
I answer'd indirectly, as I said;
And I beseech you, let not his report
Come current for an accusation
Betwixt my love and your high majesty.

Blunt. The circumstance consider'd, good my lord,   70
    Whate'er Lord Harry Percy then had said
    To such a person, and in such a place,
    At such a time, with all the rest re-told,
    May reasonably die, and never rise
    To do him wrong, or any way impeach
    What then he said, so he unsay it now.

King. Why, yet he doth deny his prisoners,
    But with proviso and exception,
    That we at our own charge shall ransom straight
    His brother-in-law, the foolish Mortimer,   80
    Who, on my soul, hath wilfully betray'd
    The lives of those that he did lead to fight
    Against that great magician, damn'd Glendower,
    Whose daughter, as we hear, the Earl of March
    Hath lately married. Shall our coffers, then,
    Be emptied, to redeem a traitor home?
    Shall we buy treason? and indent with fears,
    When they have lost and forfeited themselves?
    No, on the barren mountains let him starve;
    For I shall never hold that man my friend   90
    Whose tongue shall ask me for one penny cost

To ransom home revolted Mortimer.

Hotspur. Revolted Mortimer!
    He never did fall off, my sovereign liege,
    But by the chance of war; to prove that true
    Needs no more but one tongue for all those wounds,
    Those mouthed wounds, which valiantly he took,
    When on the gentle Severn's sedgy bank,
    In single opposition, hand to hand,
    He did confound the best part of an hour   100
    In changing hardiment with great Glendower:
    Three times they breath'd and three times did they
       drink,
    Upon agreement, of swift Severn's flood,
    Who then affrighted with their bloody looks
    Ran fearfully among the trembling reeds,
    And hid his crisp head in the hollow bank,
    Bloodstained with these valiant combatants:
    Never did bare and rotten policy
    Colour her working with such deadly wounds,
    Nor never could the noble Mortimer   110
    Receive so many, and all willingly:
    Then let not him be slander'd with revolt.

King. Thou dost belie him, Percy, thou dost belie him;
    He never did encounter with Glendower:
    I tell thee,
    He durst as well have met the devil alone
    As Owen Glendower for an enemy.
    Art thou not asham'd? But, sirrah, henceforth
    Let me not hear you speak of Mortimer:
    Send me your prisoners with the speediest means,   120
    Or you shall hear in such a kind from me
    As will displease you. My lord Northumberland,
    We license your departure with your son;
    Send us your prisoners, or you will hear of it.
                Exeunt King Henry, Blunt, and train

Hotspur. An if the devil come and roar for them,
    I will not send them: I will after straight

And tell him so, for I will ease my heart,
Albeit I make a hazard of my head.
Northumberland. What, drunk with choler? stay, and
    pause a while:
Here comes your uncle.

Re-enter Worcester

Hotspur.   Speak of Mortimer?   130
    'Zounds, I will speak of him, and let my soul
    Want mercy, if I do not join with him:
    Yea, on his part I'll empty all these veins,
    And shed my dear blood, drop by drop in the dust,
    But I will lift the down-trod Mortimer
    As high in the air as this unthankful king,
    As this ingrate and canker'd Bolingbroke.
Northumberland. Brother, the king hath made your
    nephew mad.
Worcester. Who struck this heat up after I was gone?
Hotspur. He will, forsooth, have all my prisoners,   140
    And when I urg'd the ransom once again
    Of my wife's brother, then his cheek look'd pale,
    And on my face he turn'd an eye of death,
    Trembling even at the name of Mortimer.
Worcester. I cannot blame him, was not he proclaim'd
    By Richard that dead is the next of blood?
Northumberland. He was, I heard the proclamation:
    And then it was when the unhappy king
    (Whose wrongs in us God pardon!) did set forth
    Upon his Irish expedition;   150
    From whence he intercepted did return
    To be depos'd, and shortly murdered.
Worcester. And for whose death we in the world's wide
    mouth
    Live scandaliz'd and foully spoken of.
Hotspur. But soft, I pray you, did King Richard then
    Proclaim my brother Edmund Mortimer
    Heir to the crown?

Northumberland.   He did, myself did hear it.
Hotspur. Nay then I cannot blame his cousin king,
   That wish'd him on the barren mountains starve;
   But shall it be that you, that set the crown   160
   Upon the head of this forgetful man,
   And for his sake wear the detested blot
   Of murderous subornation, shall it be
   That you a world of curses undergo,
   Being the agents, or base second means,
   The cords, the ladder, or the hangman rather—
   O pardon me, that I descend so low,
   To show the line and the predicament,
   Wherein you range under this subtle king—
   Shall it for shame be spoken in these days,   170
   Or fill up chronicles in time to come,
   That men of your nobility and power
   Did gage them both in an unjust behalf,
   (As both of you, God pardon it, have done)
   To put down Richard, that sweet lovely rose,
   And plant this thorn, this canker, Bolingbroke?
   And shall it in more shame be further spoken,
   That you are fool'd, discarded, and shook off
   By him, for whom these shames ye underwent?
   No, yet time serves, wherein you may redeem   180
   Your banish'd honours, and restore yourselves
   Into the good thoughts of the world again:
   Revenge the jeering and disdain'd contempt
   Of this proud king, who studies day and night
   To answer all the debt he owes to you
   Even with the bloody payment of your deaths:
   Therefore, I say,—
Worcester.   Peace, cousin, say no more:
   And now I will unclasp a secret book,
   And to your quick-conceiving discontents
   I'll read you matter deep and dangerous,   190
   As full of peril and adventurous spirit
   As to o'er-walk a current roaring loud,

15

On the unsteadfast footing of a spear.
Hotspur. If he fall in, good night, or sink, or swim:
 Send danger from the east unto the west,
 So honour cross it, from the north to south,
 And let them grapple: O, the blood more stirs
 To rouse a lion than to start a hare!
Northumberland. Imagination of some great exploit
 Drives him beyond the bounds of patience.   200
Hotspur. By heaven, methinks it were an easy leap,
 To pluck bright honour from the pale-fac'd moon,
 Or dive into the bottom of the deep,
 Where fathom-line could never touch the ground,
 And pluck up drowned honour by the locks,
 So he that doth redeem her thence might wear
 Without corrival all her dignities,
 But out upon this half-fac'd fellowship!
Worcester. He apprehends a world of figures here,
 But not the form of what he should attend;   210
 Good cousin, give me audience for a while.
Hotspur. I cry you mercy.
Worcester.   Those same noble Scots
 That are your prisoners,—
Hotspur.   I'll keep them all;
 By God, he shall not have a Scot of them,
 No, if a Scot would save his soul, he shall not:
 I'll keep them by this hand.
Worcester.   You start away,
 And lend no ear unto my purposes:
 Those prisoners you shall keep.
Hotspur.   Nay, I will; that's flat:
 He said he would not ransom Mortimer,
 Forbad my tongue to speak of Mortimer,   220
 But I will find him when he lies asleep,
 And in his ear I'll holla 'Mortimer!'
 Nay,
 I'll have a starling shall be taught to speak
 Nothing but 'Mortimer,' and give it him,

To keep his anger still in motion.

Worcester. Hear you, cousin, a word.

Hotspur. All studies here I solemnly defy,
    Save how to gall and pinch this Bolingbroke,
    And that same sword-and-buckler Prince of Wales,   230
    But that I think his father loves him not,
    And would be glad he met with some mischance,
    I would have him poison'd with a pot of ale.

Worcester. Farewell, kinsman; I'll talk to you
    When you are better temper'd to attend.

Northumberland. Why, what a wasp-stung and impatient
    fool
    Art thou to break into this woman's mood,
    Tying thine ear to no tongue but thine own!

Hotspur. Why, look you, I am whipp'd and scourg'd with
    rods,
    Nettled, and stung with pismires, when I hear   240
    Of this vile politician, Bolingbroke,
    In Richard's time,—what do you call the place?—
    A plague upon it, it is in Gloucestershire;
    'Twas where the madcap duke his uncle kept,
    His uncle York, where I first bow'd my knee
    Unto this king of smiles, this Bolingbroke,—
    'Sblood!—
    When you and he came back from Ravenspurgh.

Northumberland. At Berkley-castle.

Hotspur. You say true: 250
    Why, what a candy deal of courtesy
    This fawning greyhound then did proffer me,
    Look, 'when his infant fortune came to age,'
    And 'gentle Harry Percy,' and 'kind cousin;'
    O, the devil take such cozeners! God forgive me!
    Good uncle, tell your tale, I have done.

Worcester. Nay, if you have not, to it again;
    We will stay your leisure.

Hotspur.   I have done, i' faith.

Worcester. Then once more to your Scottish prisoners;

Deliver them up without their ransom straight, 260
And make the Douglas' son your only mean
For powers in Scotland, which, for divers reasons
Which I shall send you written, be assur'd,
Will easily be granted. You, my lord,

To Northumberland

Your son in Scotland being thus employ'd,
Shall secretly into the bosom creep
Of that same noble prelate well belov'd,
The archbishop.

Hotspur. Of York, is it not?

Worcester. True; who bears hard 270
His brother's death at Bristowe, the Lord Scroop.
I speak not this in estimation,
As what I think might be, but what I know
Is ruminated, plotted, and set down,
And only stays but to behold the face
Of that occasion that shall bring it on.

Hotspur. I smell it. Upon my life, it will do well.

Northumberland. Before the game is a-foot thou still let'st
slip.

Hotspur. Why, it cannot choose but be a noble plot,
And then the power of Scotland, and of York, 280
To join with Mortimer, ha?

Worcester. And so they shall.

Hotspur. In faith, it is exceedingly well aim'd.

Worcester. And 'tis no little reason bids us speed,
To save our heads by raising of a head;
For, bear ourselves as even as we can,
The king will always think him in our debt,
And think we think ourselves unsatisfied,
Till he hath found a time to pay us home:
And see already how he doth begin
To make us strangers to his looks of love. 290

Hotspur. He does, he does: we'll be reveng'd on him.

Worcester. Cousin, farewell. No further go in this
Than I by letters shall direct your course.

When time is ripe, which will be suddenly,
I'll steal to Glendower and Lord Mortimer,
Where you and Douglas and our powers at once,
As I will fashion it, shall happily meet,
To bear our fortunes in our own strong arms,
Which now we hold at much uncertainty.
Northumberland. Farewell, good brother; we shall thrive,
   I trust.   300
Hotspur. Uncle, adieu: O, let the hours be short
   Till fields, and blows, and groans, applaud our sport!
                                 Exeunt

Act Second

SCENE I

Rochester. An inn yard

Enter a Carrier with a lantern in his hand

First Car. Heigh-ho! an it be not four by the day, I'll be
   hang'd: Charles' wain is over the new chimney, and
   yet our horse not pack'd. What, ostler!
Ostler. (*within*) Anon, anon.
First Car. I prithee, Tom, beat Cut's saddle, put a few
   flocks in the point; poor jade is wrung in the withers,
   out of all cess.

Enter another Carrier

Sec. Car. Peas and beans are as dank here as a dog, and
   that is the next way to give poor jades the bots: this
   house is turn'd upside down since Robin Ostler died.   10
First Car. Poor fellow never joyed since the price of oats
   rose, it was the death of him.
Sec. Car. I think this be the most villanous house in all

London road for fleas, I am stung like a tench.

First Car. Like a tench? by the mass, there is ne'er a king
christen could be better bit than I have been since the
first cock.

Sec. Car. Why, they will allow us ne'er a jordan, and then
we leak in your chimney, and your chamber-lie breeds
fleas like a loach.   20

First Car. What, ostler! come away and be hang'd! come
away.

Sec. Car. I have a gammon of bacon, and two razes of
ginger, to be delivered as far as Charing-cross.

First Car. God's body, the turkeys in my pannier are
quite starv'd. What, ostler! A plague on thee, hast thou
never an eye in thy head? canst not hear? An 'twere
not as good deed as drink, to break the pate on thee,
I am a very villain. Come and be hang'd! hast no faith
in thee?   30

Enter Gadshill

Gadshill. Good morrow, carriers; what's o'clock?

First Car. I think it be two o'clock.

Gadshill. I prithee, lend me thy lantern, to see my gelding in the stable.

First Car. Nay, by God, soft, I know a trick worth two   †
of that, i' faith.

Gadshill. I pray thee, lend me thine.

Sec. Car. Ay, when? canst tell? Lend me thy lantern,
quoth he? marry, I'll see thee hang'd first.

Gadshill. Sirrah carrier, what time do you mean to come   40
to London?

Sec. Car. Time enough to go to bed with a candle, I
warrant thee. Come, neighbour Mugs, we'll call up the
gentlemen: they will along with company, for they
have great charge.   *Exeunt Carriers*

Gadshill. What ho! chamberlain!

Chamberlain. (*within*) At hand, quoth pick-purse.

Gadshill. That's even as fair as—at hand, quoth the cham-

berlain; for thou variest no more from picking of purses
than giving direction doth from labouring; thou layest   50
the plot how.

Enter Chamberlain

Chamberlain. Good morrow, Master Gadshill. It holds
current that I told you yesternight, there's a franklin
in the weald of Kent hath brought three hundred
marks with him in gold; I heard him tell it to one of
his company last night at supper, a kind of auditor, one
that hath abundance of charge too, God knows what;
they are up already, and call for eggs and butter; they
will away presently.

Gadshill. Sirrah, if they meet not with Saint Nicholas'   60
clerks, I'll give thee this neck.

Chamberlain. No, I'll none of it: I pray thee keep that for
the hangman, for I know thou worshippest Saint Nicholas, as truly as a man of falsehood may.

Gadshill. What talkest thou to me of the hangman? if I
hang, I'll make a fat pair of gallows: for if I hang, old
Sir John hangs with me, and thou knowest he is no
starveling. Tut! there are other Trojans that thou
dream'st not of, the which for sport sake are content
to do the profession some grace, that would, if mat-   70
ters should be look'd into, for their own credit sake
make all whole. I am join'd with no foot land-rakers,
no long-staff sixpenny strikers, none of these mad mus-
tachio purple-hued malt-worms, but with nobility and
tranquillity, burgomasters and great oneyers, such as   †
can hold in, such as will strike sooner than speak, and
speak sooner than drink, and drink sooner than pray,
and yet, 'zounds, I lie, for they pray continually to
their saint, the commonwealth, or rather, not pray to
her, but prey on her, for they ride up and down on her,   80
and make her their boots.

Chamberlain. What, the commonwealth their boots? will
she hold out water in foul way?

21

Gadshill. She will, she will, justice hath liquor'd her. We
steal as in a castle, cock-sure; we have the receipt of
fern-seed, we walk invisible.

Chamberlain. Nay, by my faith, I think you are more be-
holding to the night than to fern-seed for your walk-
ing invisible.

Gadshill. Give me thy hand, thou shalt have a share in   90
our purchase, as I am a true man.

Chamberlain. Nay, rather let me have it, as you are a
false thief.

Gadshill. Go to; 'homo' is a common name to all men:
bid the ostler bring my gelding out of the stable; farewell, you muddy knave.   *Exeunt*

SCENE II

The highway, near Gadshill

Enter Prince Henry and Poins

Poins. Come, shelter, shelter; I have remov'd Falstaff's
horse, and he frets like a gumm'd velvet.

Prince. Stand close.

Enter Falstaff

Falstaff. Poins, Poins, and be hanged, Poins!

Prince. Peace, ye fat-kidney'd rascal, what a brawling dost
thou keep?

Falstaff. Where's Poins, Hal?

Prince. He is walk'd up to the top of the hill; I'll go seek
him.

Falstaff. I am accurs'd to rob in that thief's company: the   10
rascal hath removed my horse, and tied him I know
not where; if I travel but four foot by the squire further afoot, I shall break my wind. Well, I doubt not
but to die a fair death for all this, if I 'scape hanging for
killing that rogue. I have forsworn his company hourly
any time this two and twenty years, and yet I am be-

22

witch'd with the rogue's company. If the rascal have
not given me medicines to make me love him, I'll be
hang'd. It could not be else; I have drunk medicines.
Poins! Hal! a plague upon you both! Bardolph! Peto!   20
I'll starve ere I'll rob a foot further. An 'twere not as
good a deed as drink to turn true man, and to leave
these rogues, I am the veriest varlet that ever chewed
with a tooth. Eight yards of uneven ground is three-
score and ten miles afoot with me, and the stony-
hearted villains know it well enough, a plague upon it
when thieves cannot be true one to another! (*They
whistle.*) Whew! A plague upon you all, give me my
horse, you rogues, give me my horse, and be hang'd!

Prince. Peace, ye fat-guts! lie down, lay thine ear close to   30
the ground, and list if thou canst hear the tread of
travellers.

Falstaff. Have you any levers to lift me up again being
down? 'Sblood, I'll not bear mine own flesh so far afoot
again for all the coin in thy father's exchequer. What
a plague mean ye to colt me thus?

Prince. Thou liest; thou art not colted, thou art uncolted.

Falstaff. I prithee, good prince, Hal, help me to my horse,
good king's son.

Prince. Out, ye rogue! shall I be your ostler?   40

Falstaff. Go hang thyself in thine own heir-apparent gar-
ters! If I be ta'en, I'll peach for this. An I have not
ballads made on you all, and sung to filthy tunes, let
a cup of sack be my poison: when a jest is so forward,
and afoot too! I hate it.

Enter Gadshill, Bardolph and Peto with him

Gadshill. Stand.

Falstaff. So I do, against my will.

Poins. O, 'tis our setter, I know his voice. Bardolph, what
news?

Bardolph. Case ye, case ye, on with your vizards; there's   50

23

money of the king's coming down the hill, 'tis going
to the king's exchequer.

Falstaff. You lie, ye rogue; 'tis going to the king's tavern.

Gadshill. There's enough to make us all.

Falstaff. To be hang'd.

Prince. Sirs,
    You four shall front them in the narrow lane;
    Ned Poins and I will walk lower; if they 'scape
    From your encounter, then they light on us.

Peto. How many be there of them?   60

Gadshill. Some eight or ten.

Falstaff. 'Zounds, will they not rob us?

Prince. What, a coward, Sir John Paunch?

Falstaff. Indeed, I am not John of Gaunt, your grandfather, but yet no coward, Hal.

Prince. Well, we leave that to the proof.

Poins. Sirrah Jack, thy horse stands behind the hedge;
when thou need'st him, there thou shalt find him: farewell, and stand fast.

Falstaff. Now cannot I strike him, if I should be hang'd.   70

Prince. Ned, where are our disguises?

Poins. Here, hard by, stand close.

                          Exeunt Prince and Poins

Falstaff. Now, my masters, happy man be his dole, say I:
every man to his business.

               Enter the Travellers

First Trav. Come, neighbour, the boy shall lead our
horses down the hill, we'll walk afoot awhile, and ease
our legs.

Thieves. Stand!

Travellers. Jesus bless us!

Falstaff. Strike, down with them, cut the villains' throats: 80
ah! whoreson caterpillars, bacon-fed knaves! they hate
us youth, down with them, fleece them.

Travellers. O, we are undone, both we and ours for ever!

Falstaff. Hang ye, gorbellied knaves, are ye undone? No,
ye fat chuffs, I would your store were here! On, bacons,

on! What, ye knaves? young men must live; you are
grandjurors, are ye? we'll jure ye, 'faith.

Here they rob them and bind them. Exeunt

Re-enter Prince Henry and Poins disguised

Prince. The thieves have bound the true men; now could
thou and I rob the thieves, and go merrily to London,
it would be argument for a week, laughter for a month,   90
and a good jest for ever.

Poins. Stand close, I hear them coming.

Enter the Thieves again

Falstaff. Come, my masters, let us share, and then to horse
before day; an the Prince and Poins be not two arrant
cowards, there's no equity stirring: there's no more
valour in that Poins than in a wild-duck.

Prince. Your money!

Poins. Villains!

> *As they are sharing, the Prince and Poins set
> upon them; they all run away; and Falstaff,
> after a blow or two, runs away too, leaving the
> booty behind them.*

Prince. Got with much ease. Now merrily to horse:
The thieves are all scatter'd and possess'd with fear   100
So strongly that they dare not meet each other;
Each takes his fellow for an officer.
Away, good Ned. Falstaff sweats to death,
And lards the lean earth as he walks along:
Were 't not for laughing, I should pity him.

Poins. How the rogue roar'd!   *Exeunt*

SCENE III

Warkworth Castle

Enter Hotspur solus, reading a letter

Hotspur. 'But, for mine own part, my lord, I could be well
contented to be there, in respect of the love I bear your

25

house.' He could be contented: why is he not, then?
In respect of the love he bears our house: he shows in
this, he loves his own barn better than he loves our
house. Let me see some more. 'The purpose you undertake is dangerous;'—why, that's certain: 'tis dangerous
to take a cold, to sleep, to drink; but I tell you, my lord
fool, out of this nettle danger, we pluck this flower
safety. 'The purpose you undertake is dangerous, the   10
friends you have named uncertain, the time itself unsorted, and your whole plot too light, for the counter-
poise of so great an opposition.' Say you so, say you so,
I say unto you again, you are a shallow cowardly hind,
and you lie. What a lack-brain is this! By the Lord, our
plot is a good plot as ever was laid, our friends true
and constant: a good plot, good friends, and full of expectation; an excellent plot, very good friends. What a
frosty-spirited rogue is this! Why, my lord of York
commends the plot, and the general course of the ac-   20
tion. 'Zounds, an I were now by this rascal, I could
brain him with his lady's fan. Is there not my father, my
uncle, and myself; lord Edmund Mortimer, my lord of
York, and Owen Glendower; is there not besides the
Douglas, have I not all their letters to meet me in arms
by the ninth of the next month, and are they not some
of them set forward already? What a pagan rascal is
this, an infidel! Ha! you shall see now in very sincerity
of fear and cold heart, will he to the king, and lay open
all our proceedings. O, I could divide myself, and go   †
to buffets, for moving such a dish of skim milk with so   31
honourable an action! Hang him! let him tell the king:
we are prepared. I will set forward to-night.

Enter Lady Percy

How now, Kate! I must leave you within these two
   hours.
Lady Percy. O, my good lord, why are you thus alone?
For what offence have I this fortnight been

A banish'd woman from my Harry's bed?
Tell me, sweet lord, what is 't that takes from thee
Thy stomach, pleasure, and thy golden sleep?
Why dost thou bend thine eyes upon the earth?   40
And start so often when thou sit'st alone?
Why hast thou lost the fresh blood in thy cheeks?
And given my treasures and my rights of thee
To thick-ey'd musing, and curs'd melancholy?
In thy faint slumbers I by thee have watch'd,
And heard thee murmur tales of iron wars,
Speak terms of manage to thy bounding steed,
Cry 'Courage! to the field!' And thou hast talk'd
Of sallies and retires, of trenches, tents,
Of palisadoes, frontiers, parapets,   50
Of basilisks, of cannon, culverin,
Of prisoners' ransom, and of soldiers slain,
And all the currents of a heady fight;
Thy spirit within thee hath been so at war,
And thus hath so bestirr'd thee in thy sleep,
That beads of sweat have stood upon thy brow,
Like bubbles in a late-disturbed stream,
And in thy face strange motions have appear'd,
Such as we see when men restrain their breath,
On some great sudden hest. O, what portents are
   these?   60
Some heavy business hath my lord in hand,
And I must know it, else he loves me not.
Hotspur. What ho!

Enter Servant

       Is Gilliams with the packet gone?
Servant. He is, my lord, an hour ago.
Hotspur. Hath Butler brought those horses from the
   sheriff?
Servant. One horse, my lord, he brought even now.
Hotspur. What horse? Roan, a crop-ear, is it not?
Servant. It is, my lord.

27

Hotspur.   That roan shall be my throne.
  Well, I will back him straight: O esperance!
  Bid Butler lead him forth into the park.   *Exit Servant*   70
Lady Percy. But hear you, my lord.
Hotspur. What say'st thou, my lady?
Lady Percy. What is it carries you away?
Hotspur. Why, my horse, my love, my horse.
Lady Percy. Out, you mad-headed ape!
  A weasel hath not such a deal of spleen
  As you are toss'd with. In faith,
  I'll know your business, Harry, that I will.
  I fear my brother Mortimer doth stir
  About his title, and hath sent for you   80
  To line his enterprize: but if you go—
Hotspur. So far afoot, I shall be weary, love.
Lady Percy. Come, come, you paraquito, answer me
  Directly unto this question that I ask:
  In faith, I'll break thy little finger, Harry,
  An if thou wilt not tell me all things true.
Hotspur. Away,
  Away, you trifler! Love, I love thee not,
  I care not for thee, Kate, this is no world
  To play with mammets and to tilt with lips,   90
  We must have bloody noses, and crack'd crowns,
  And pass them current too. God's me, my horse!
  What say'st thou, Kate? what wouldst thou have with
    me?
Lady Percy. Do you not love me? do you not, indeed?
  Well, do not then, for since you love me not,
  I will not love myself. Do you not love me?
  Nay, tell me if you speak in jest or no.
Hotspur. Come, wilt thou see me ride?
  And when I am a horseback, I will swear
  I love thee infinitely. But hark you, Kate;   100
  I must not have you henceforth question me
  Whither I go, nor reason whereabout:
  Whither I must, I must, and, to conclude,

This evening must I leave you, gentle Kate.
I know you wise, but yet no farther wise
Than Harry Percy's wife: constant you are,
But yet a woman: and for secrecy,
No lady closer, for I well believe
Thou wilt not utter what thou dost not know;
And so far will I trust thee, gentle Kate.   110
Lady Percy. How? so far?
Hotspur. Not an inch further; but hark you, Kate:
Whither I go, thither shall you go too;
To-day will I set forth, to-morrow you.
Will this content you, Kate?
Lady Percy.   It must of force.   *Exeunt*

SCENE IV

The Boar's-Head Tavern in Eastcheap

Enter the Prince, and Poins

Prince. Ned, prithee come out of that fat room, and lend
me thy hand to laugh a little.
Poins. Where hast been, Hal?
Prince. With three or four loggerheads, amongst three or
fourscore hogsheads. I have sounded the very base-
string of humility. Sirrah, I am sworn brother to a leash
of drawers, and can call them all by their christen
names, as Tom, Dick, and Francis. They take it already upon their salvation, that though I be but Prince
of Wales, yet I am the king of courtesy, and tell me   10
flatly I am no proud Jack, like Falstaff, but a Corinthian, a lad of mettle, a good boy (by the Lord, so they
call me) and when I am king of England, I shall command all the good lads in Eastcheap. They call drinking deep, dyeing scarlet, and when you breathe in your
watering, they cry 'hem!' and bid you play it off. To
conclude, I am so good a proficient in one quarter of
an hour, that I can drink with any tinker in his own
language during my life. I tell thee, Ned, thou hast lost

29

much honour, that thou wert not with me in this action.   20
But, sweet Ned,—to sweeten which name of Ned, I give
thee this pennyworth of sugar, clapp'd even now into
my hand by an under-skinker, one that never spake
other English in his life than 'Eight shillings and six-
pence,' and 'You are welcome,' with this shrill addition,
'Anon, anon, sir! Score a pint of bastard in the Half-
moon,' or so. But, Ned, to drive away the time till Falstaff come, I prithee, do thou stand in some by-room,
while I question my puny drawer to what end he gave
me the sugar, and do thou never leave calling 'Francis,'   30
that his tale to me may be nothing but 'Anon.' Step
aside, and I'll show thee a precedent.

Poins. Francis!

Prince. Thou art perfect.

Poins. Francis!   *Exit Poins*

Enter Francis

Francis. Anon, anon, sir. Look down into the Pomgarnet,
Ralph.

Prince. Come hither, Francis.

Francis. My lord?

Prince. How long hast thou to serve, Francis?   40

Francis. Forsooth, five years, and as much as to—

Poins. (*within*) Francis!

Francis. Anon, anon, sir.

Prince. Five year! by 'r lady, a long lease for the clinking
of pewter. But, Francis, darest thou be so valiant as to
play the coward with thy indenture, and show it a fair
pair of heels, and run from it?

Francis. O Lord, sir, I'll be sworn upon all the books in
England, I could find in my heart.

Poins. (*within*) Francis!   50

Francis. Anon, sir.

Prince. How old art thou, Francis?

Francis. Let me see—about Michaelmas next I shall be—

Poins. (*within*) Francis!

Francis. Anon, sir, pray stay a little, my lord.

Prince. Nay, but hark you, Francis: for the sugar thou
gavest me, 'twas a pennyworth, was 't not?

Francis. O Lord, I would it had been two!

Prince. I will give thee for it a thousand pound: ask me
when thou wilt, and thou shalt have it.   60

Poins. (*within*) Francis!

Francis. Anon, anon.

Prince. Anon, Francis? No, Francis; but to-morrow, Francis; or Francis, o' Thursday; or indeed, Francis, when
thou wilt. But, Francis!

Francis. My lord?

Prince. Wilt thou rob this leathern jerkin, crystal-button,
not-pated, agate-ring, puke-stocking, caddis-garter,
smooth-tongue, Spanish pouch?

Francis. O lord, sir, who do you mean?   70

Prince. Why, then, your brown bastard is your only
drink; for look you, Francis, your white canvas doublet
will sully; in Barbary, sir, it cannot come to so much.

Francis. What, sir?

Poins. (*within*) Francis!

Prince. Away, you rogue! dost thou not hear them call?
            *Here they both call him; the drawer stands
                  amazed, not knowing which way to go*

Enter Vintner

Vintner. What, stand'st thou still, and hear'st such a calling? Look to the guests within. (*exit Francis.*) My lord,
old Sir John with half-a-dozen more are at the door:
shall I let them in?   80

Prince. Let them alone awhile, and then open the door.
(*exit Vintner.*) Poins!

Re-enter Poins

Poins. Anon, anon, sir.

Prince. Sirrah, Falstaff and the rest of the thieves are at
the door: shall we be merry?

31

Poins. As merry as crickets, my lad. But hark ye, what cunning match have you made with this jest of the drawer? come, what's the issue?

Prince. I am now of all humours, that have showed themselves humours since the old days of goodman Adam to   90
the pupil age of this present twelve o'clock at midnight.

What's o'clock, Francis?

Francis. Anon, anon, sir.

Prince. That ever this fellow should have fewer words than a parrot, and yet the son of a woman! His industry is up-stairs and down-stairs, his eloquence the parcel of a reckoning. I am not yet of Percy's mind, the Hotspur of the north, he that kills me some six or seven dozen of Scots at a breakfast; washes his hands, and   100
says to his wife 'Fie upon this quiet life! I want work.' 'O my sweet Harry,' says she, 'how many hast thou kill'd to-day?' 'Give my roan horse a drench,' says he; and answers 'some fourteen,' an hour after; 'a trifle, a trifle.' I prithee, call in Falstaff: I'll play Percy, and that damn'd brawn shall play Dame Mortimer his wife. 'Rivo!' says the drunkard. Call in ribs, call in tallow.

Enter Falstaff, Gadshill, Bardolph, and Peto;
Francis following with wine

Poins. Welcome, Jack: where hast thou been?

Falstaff. A plague of all cowards, I say, and a vengeance too, marry and amen! Give me a cup of sack, boy. Ere   110
I lead this life long, I'll sew nether stocks and mend them and foot them too. A plague of all cowards! Give me a cup of sack, rogue. Is there no virtue extant?

He drinks

Prince. Didst thou never see Titan kiss a dish of butter? pitiful-hearted butter, that melted at the sweet tale of   †
the sun's! if thou didst, then behold that compound.

Falstaff. You rogue, here's lime in this sack too: there is nothing but roguery to be found in villanous man: yet

32

a coward is worse than a cup of sack with lime in it.
A villanous coward! Go thy ways, old Jack, die when   120
thou wilt, if manhood, good manhood, be not forgot
upon the face of the earth, then am I a shotten her-
ring. There lives not three good men unhang'd in England, and one of them is fat, and grows old, God help
the while! a bad world, I say, I would I were a weaver;
I could sing psalms or any thing. A plague of all cowards, I say still.

Prince. How now, wool-sack, what mutter you?

Falstaff. A king's son! If I do not beat thee out of thy
kingdom with a dagger of lath, and drive all thy sub-   130
jects afore thee like a flock of wild-geese, I'll never
wear hair on my face more, you Prince of Wales!

Prince. Why, you whoreson round man, what's the
matter?

Falstaff. Are not you a coward? answer me to that, and
Poins there?

Poins. 'Zounds, ye fat paunch, an ye call me coward, by
the Lord, I'll stab thee.

Falstaff. I call thee coward? I'll see thee damn'd ere I call
thee coward, but I would give a thousand pound I   140
could run as fast as thou canst. You are straight enough
in the shoulders, you care not who sees your back: call
you that backing of your friends? A plague upon such
backing! give me them that will face me, give me a
cup of sack: I am a rogue, if I drunk to-day.

Prince. O villain! thy lips are scarce wip'd since thou
drunk'st last.

Falstaff. All is one for that. (*He drinks.*) A plague of all
cowards, still say I.

Prince. What's the matter?   150

Falstaff. What's the matter? there be four of us here have
ta'en a thousand pound this day morning.

Prince. Where is it, Jack, where is it?

Falstaff. Where is it? taken from us it is: a hundred upon
poor four of us.

33

Prince. What, a hundred, man?

Falstaff. I am a rogue, if I were not at half-sword with a dozen of them two hours together. I have 'scap'd by miracle. I am eight times thrust through the doublet, four through the hose, my buckler cut through and through, my sword hack'd like a handsaw—*ecce signum*! I never dealt better since I was a man: all would not do. A plague of all cowards! Let them speak: if they speak more or less than truth, they are villains, and the sons of darkness. 160

Prince. Speak, sirs, how was it?

Gadshill. We four set upon some dozen—

Falstaff. Sixteen at least, my lord.

Gadshill. And bound them.

Peto. No, no, they were not bound. 170

Falstaff. You rogue, they were bound, every man of them, or I am a Jew else; an Ebrew Jew.

Gadshill. As we were sharing, some six or seven fresh men set upon us—

Falstaff. And unbound the rest, and then come in the other.

Prince. What, fought you with them all?

Falstaff. All? I know not what you call all; but if I fought not with fifty of them, I am a bunch of radish: if there were not two or three and fifty upon poor old Jack, then am I no two-legg'd creature. 180

Prince. Pray God you have not murder'd some of them.

Falstaff. Nay, that's past praying for: I have pepper'd two of them; two I am sure I have paid, two rogues in buckram suits. I tell thee what, Hal, if I tell thee a lie, spit in my face, call me horse; thou knowest my old ward; here I lay, and thus I bore my point, four rogues in buckram let drive at me—

Prince. What, four? thou saidst but two even now.

Falstaff. Four, Hal, I told thee four. 190

Poins. Ay, ay, he said four.

Falstaff. These four came all a-front, and mainly thrust

34

at me, I made me no more ado, but took all their seven
points in my target, thus.

Prince. Seven? why, there were but four even now.

Falstaff. In buckram?

Poins. Ay, four, in buckram suits.

Falstaff. Seven, by these hilts, or I am a villain else.

Prince. Prithee let him alone, we shall have more anon.

Falstaff. Dost thou hear me, Hal?   200

Prince. Ay, and mark thee too, Jack.

Falstaff. Do so, for it is worth the listening to; these nine
in buckram that I told thee of,—

Prince. So, two more already.

Falstaff. Their points being broken,—

Poins. Down fell their hose.

Falstaff. Began to give me ground: but I followed me
close, came in foot and hand, and with a thought seven
of the eleven I paid.

Prince. O monstrous! eleven buckram men grown out of   210
two!

Falstaff. But, as the devil would have it, three misbe-
gotten knaves in Kendal green came at my back, and
let drive at me, for it was so dark, Hal, that thou
couldst not see thy hand.

Prince. These lies are like their father that begets them,
Gross as a mountain, open, palpable.
Why, thou clay-brain'd guts, thou knotty-pated fool,
Thou whoreson obscene greasy tallow-catch,—

Falstaff. What, art thou mad? art thou mad? is not the   220
truth the truth?

Prince. Why, how couldst thou know these men in
Kendal green, when it was so dark thou couldst not see
thy hand? come, tell us your reason. What sayest thou
to this?

Poins. Come, your reason, Jack, your reason.

Falstaff. What, upon compulsion? 'Zounds, an I were at
the strappado, or all the racks in the world, I would
not tell you on compulsion. Give you a reason on

35

compulsion? if reasons were as plentiful as black- 230
berries, I would give no man a reason upon compulsion, I.

Prince. I'll be no longer guilty of this sin;
This sanguine coward, this bed-presser,
This horseback-breaker, this huge hill of flesh,—

Falstaff. 'Sblood, you starveling, you elf-skin, you dried
neat's tongue, you bull's pizzle, you stock-fish! O for
breath to utter what is like thee, you tailor's-yard, you
sheath, you bow-case, you vile standing-tuck,—

Prince. Well, breathe a while, and then to it again, and 240
when thou hast tired thyself in base comparisons, hear
me speak but this.

Poins. Mark, Jack.

Prince. We two saw you four set on four and bound them,
and were masters of their wealth. Mark now how a
plain tale shall put you down; then did we two set on
you four, and, with a word, out-fac'd you from your
prize, and have it, yea, and can show it you here in the
house: and, Falstaff, you carried your guts away as
nimbly, with as quick dexterity, and roar'd for mercy, 250
and still run and roar'd, as ever I heard bull-calf.
What a slave art thou, to hack thy sword as thou hast
done; and then say it was in fight! What trick, what
device, what starting-hole, canst thou now find out, to
hide thee from this open and apparent shame?

Poins. Come, let's hear, Jack, what trick hast thou now?

Falstaff. By the Lord, I knew ye as well as he that made
ye. Why, hear you, my masters, was it for me to kill the
heir-apparent? should I turn upon the true prince?
why, thou knowest I am as valiant as Hercules: but 260
beware instinct, the lion will not touch the true prince,
instinct is a great matter; I was now a coward on instinct. I shall think the better of myself and thee during
my life; I for a valiant lion, and thou for a true prince.
But, by the Lord, lads, I am glad you have the money;
hostess, clap to the doors, watch to-night, pray to-

morrow, gallants, lads, boys, hearts of gold, all the
titles of good fellowship come to you! What, shall we
be merry? shall we have a play extempore?

Prince. Content, and the argument shall be thy running   270
away.

Falstaff. Ah, no more of that, Hal, an thou lovest me!

Enter Mistress Quickly

Quickly. O Jesu, my lord the prince!

Prince. How now, my lady the hostess, what say'st thou
to me?

Quickly. Marry, my lord, there is a nobleman of the court
at door would speak with you: he says he comes from
your father.

Prince. Give him as much as will make him a royal man,
and send him back again to my mother.   280

Falstaff. What manner of man is he?

Quickly. An old man.

Falstaff. What doth gravity out of his bed at midnight?
Shall I give him his answer?

Prince. Prithee, do, Jack.

Falstaff. Faith, and I'll send him packing.   *Exit*

Prince. Now, sirs, by 'r lady, you fought fair, so did you,
Peto, so did you, Bardolph: you are lions too, you ran
away upon instinct, you will not touch the true prince;
no, fie!   290

Bardolph. Faith, I ran when I saw others run.

Prince. Faith, tell me now in earnest, how came Falstaff's
sword so hack'd?

Peto. Why, he hack'd it with his dagger, and said he
would swear truth out of England, but he would make
you believe it was done in fight, and persuaded us to
do the like.

Bardolph. Yea, and to tickle our noses with spear-grass,
to make them bleed, and then to beslubber our garments with it, and swear it was the blood of true men.   300

37

I did that I did not this seven year before, I blush'd
to hear his monstrous devices.

Prince. O villain, thou stolest a cup of sack eighteen
years ago, and wert taken with the manner, and ever
since thou hast blush'd extempore. Thou hadst fire and
sword on thy side, and yet thou ran'st away: what
instinct hadst thou for it?

Bardolph. My lord, do you see these meteors? do you
behold these exhalations?

Prince. I do. 310

Bardolph. What think you they portend?

Prince. Hot livers and cold purses.

Bardolph. Choler, my lord, if rightly taken.

Prince. No, if rightly taken, halter.

Re-enter Falstaff

Here comes lean Jack, here comes bare-bone. How
now, my sweet creature of bombast, how long is 't
ago, Jack, since thou sawest thine own knee?

Falstaff. My own knee? when I was about thy years, Hal,
I was not an eagle's talon in the waist, I could have
crept into any alderman's thumb-ring: a plague of 320
sighing and grief, it blows a man up like a bladder.
There's villanous news abroad: here was Sir John
Bracy from your father; you must to the court in the
morning. That same mad fellow of the north, Percy,
and he of Wales, that gave Amamon the bastinado
and made Lucifer cuckold, and swore the devil his
true liegeman upon the cross of a Welsh hook—what
a plague call you him?

Poins. O, Glendower.

Falstaff. Owen, Owen, the same, and his son-in-law 330
Mortimer, and old Northumberland, and that sprightly
Scot of Scots, Douglas, that runs a horseback up a hill
perpendicular,—

Prince. He that rides at high speed and with his pistol
kills a sparrow flying.

Falstaff. You have hit it.

Prince. So did he never the sparrow.

Falstaff. Well, that rascal hath good mettle in him, he will
not run.

Prince. Why, what a rascal art thou then, to praise him   340
so for running!

Falstaff. A horseback, ye cuckoo, but afoot he will not
budge a foot.

Prince. Yes, Jack, upon instinct.

Falstaff. I grant ye, upon instinct. Well, he is there too,
and one Mordake, and a thousand blue-caps more:
Worcester is stolen away to-night, thy father's beard
is turn'd white with the news, you may buy land now
as cheap as stinking mackerel.

Prince. Why, then, it is like, if there come a hot June,   350
and this civil buffeting hold, we shall buy maidenheads
as they buy hob-nails, by the hundreds.

Falstaff. By the mass, lad, thou sayest true, it is like we
shall have good trading that way. But tell me, Hal, art
not thou horrible afeard? thou being heir-apparent,
could the world pick thee out three such enemies
again as that fiend Douglas, that spirit Percy, and that
devil Glendower? art thou not horribly afraid? doth
not thy blood thrill at it?

Prince. Not a whit, i' faith; I lack some of thy instinct.   360

Falstaff. Well, thou wilt be horribly chid to-morrow when
thou comest to thy father: if thou love me, practise an
answer.

Prince. Do thou stand for my father, and examine me
upon the particulars of my life.

Falstaff. Shall I? content. This chair shall be my state, this
dagger my sceptre, and this cushion my crown.

Prince. Thy state is taken for a joined-stool, thy golden
sceptre for a leaden dagger, and thy precious rich
crown for a pitiful bald crown!   370

Falstaff. Well, an the fire of grace be not quite out of
thee, now shalt thou be moved. Give me a cup of sack

39

to make my eyes look red, that it may be thought I
have wept, for I must speak in passion, and I will do
it in King Cambyses' vein.

Prince. Well, here is my leg.

Falstaff. And here is my speech. Stand aside, nobility.

Quickly. O Jesu, this is excellent sport, i' faith!

Falstaff. Weep not, sweet queen, for trickling tears are
vain.   380

Quickly. O, the father, how he holds his countenance!

Falstaff. For God's sake, lords, convey my tristful queen,
For tears do stop the flood-gates of her eyes.

Quickly. O Jesu, he doth it as like one of these harlotry
players as ever I see!

Falstaff. Peace, good pint-pot, peace, good tickle-brain.
Harry, I do not only marvel where thou spendest thy
time, but also how thou art accompanied. For though
the camomile, the more it is trodden on, the faster it
grows; so youth, the more it is wasted, the sooner it   †
wears. That thou art my son I have partly thy mother's   391
word, partly my own opinion, but chiefly a villanous
trick of thine eye, and a foolish hanging of thy nether
lip, that doth warrant me. If then thou be son to me,
here lies the point, why, being son to me, art thou so
pointed at? Shall the blessed sun of heaven prove a
micher, and eat blackberries? a question not to be
ask'd. Shall the son of England prove a thief, and take
purses? a question to be ask'd. There is a thing, Harry,
which thou hast often heard of, and it is known to   400
many in our land by the name of pitch. This pitch (as
ancient writers do report) doth defile, so doth the
company thou keepest: for, Harry, now I do not speak
to thee in drink, but in tears; not in pleasure but in
passion; not in words only, but in woes also: and yet
there is a virtuous man whom I have often noted in thy
company, but I know not his name.

Prince. What manner of man, an it like your majesty?

Falstaff. A goodly portly man, i' faith, and a corpulent, of
a cheerful look, a pleasing eye, and a most noble car-   410
riage, and, as I think, his age some fifty, or, by 'r lady,
inclining to three score, and now I remember me, his
name is Falstaff, if that man should be lewdly given,
he deceiveth me. For, Harry, I see virtue in his looks:
if then the tree may be known by the fruit, as the fruit
by the tree, then peremptorily I speak it, there is virtue
in that Falstaff, him keep with, the rest banish, and
tell me now, thou naughty varlet, tell me, where hast
thou been this month?

Prince. Dost thou speak like a king? Do thou stand for   420
me, and I'll play my father.

Falstaff. Depose me? if thou dost it half so gravely, so
majestically, both in word and matter, hang me up by
the heels for a rabbit-sucker, or a poulter's hare.

Prince. Well, here I am set.

Falstaff. And here I stand: judge, my masters.

Prince. Now, Harry, whence come you?

Falstaff. My noble lord, from Eastcheap.

Prince. The complaints I hear of thee are grievous.

Falstaff. 'Sblood, my lord, they are false: nay, I'll tickle   430
ye for a young prince, i' faith.

Prince. Swearest thou, ungracious boy? henceforth ne'er   †
look on me. Thou art violently carried away from
grace, there is a devil haunts thee in the likeness of
an old fat man, a tun of man is thy companion: why
dost thou converse with that trunk of humours, that
bolting-hutch of beastliness, that swollen parcel of
dropsies, that huge bombard of sack, that stuff'd cloak-
bag of guts, that roasted Manningtree ox with the pud-
ding in his belly, that reverend vice, that grey iniquity,   440
that father ruffian, that vanity in years? Wherein is he
good, but to taste sack and drink it? wherein neat and
cleanly, but to carve a capon and eat it? wherein cunning, but in craft? wherein crafty, but in villany?

41

wherein villanous, but in all things? wherein worthy,
but in nothing?

Falstaff. I would your grace would take me with you,
whom means your grace?

Prince. That villanous abominable misleader of youth,
Falstaff, that old white-bearded Satan.   450

Falstaff. My lord, the man I know.

Prince. I know thou dost.

Falstaff. But to say I know more harm in him than in
myself, were to say more than I know: that he is old
(the more the pity) his white hairs do witness it, but
that he is, saving your reverence, a whoremaster, that
I utterly deny: if sack and sugar be a fault, God help
the wicked! if to be old and merry be a sin, then many
an old host that I know is damn'd: if to be fat be to be
hated, then Pharaoh's lean kine are to be loved. No,   460
my good lord; banish Peto, banish Bardolph, banish
Poins, but for sweet Jack Falstaff, kind Jack Falstaff,
true Jack Falstaff, valiant Jack Falstaff, and therefore
more valiant, being, as he is, old Jack Falstaff, banish
not him thy Harry's company, banish not him thy
Harry's company, banish plump Jack, and banish all
the world.

Prince. I do, I will.   *A knocking heard*
Exeunt Mistress Quickly, Francis, and Bardolph

Re-enter Bardolph, running

Bardolph. O, my lord, my lord! the sheriff with a most
monstrous watch is at the door.   470

Falstaff. Out, ye rogue! Play out the play: I have much
to say in the behalf of that Falstaff.

Re-enter Mistress Quickly

Quickly. O Jesu, my lord, my lord!—

Prince. Heigh, heigh! the devil rides upon a fiddle-stick,
what's the matter?

Quickly. The sheriff and all the watch are at the door, they are come to search the house, shall I let them in?

Falstaff. Dost thou hear, Hal? never call a true piece of gold a counterfeit: thou art essentially made, without seeming so.   †
480

Prince. And thou a natural coward, without instinct.

Falstaff. I deny your major: if you will deny the sheriff, so; if not, let him enter: if I become not a cart as well as another man, a plague on my bringing up! I hope I shall as soon be strangled with a halter as another.

Prince. Go hide thee behind the arras, the rest walk up above. Now, my masters, for a true face, and good conscience.

Falstaff. Both which I have had, but their date is out, and therefore I'll hide me.   490

Prince. Call in the sheriff.

Exeunt all except the Prince and Peto

Enter Sheriff and the Carrier

Now, master sheriff, what is your will with me?

Sheriff. First pardon me, my lord. A hue and cry
Hath follow'd certain men unto this house.

Prince. What men?

Sheriff. One of them is well known, my gracious lord,
A gross fat man.

Car.   As fat as butter.

Prince. The man, I do assure you, is not here,
For I myself at this time have employ'd him.
And, sheriff, I will engage my word to thee   500
That I will by to-morrow dinner-time
Send him to answer thee or any man,
For any thing he shall be charg'd withal,
And so let me entreat you leave the house.

Sheriff. I will, my lord. There are two gentlemen
Have in this robbery lost three hundred marks.

Prince. It may be so: if he have robb'd these men,
He shall be answerable, and so farewell.

43

Sheriff. Good night, my noble lord.

Prince. I think it is good morrow, is it not? 510

Sheriff. Indeed, my lord, I think it be two o'clock.

Exeunt Sheriff and Carrier

Prince. This oily rascal is known as well as Paul's.
  Go, call him forth.

Peto. Falstaff!—Fast asleep behind the arras, and snorting like a horse.

Prince. Hark how hard he fetches breath; search his pockets. (*He searcheth his pockets, and findeth certain papers.*) What hast thou found?

Peto. Nothing but papers, my lord.

Prince. Let's see what they be: read them. 520

Peto. (*reads*) Item a capon, . . 2s. 2d.
  Item sauce, . . 4d.
  Item sack two gallons, 5s. 8d.
  Item anchovies and
    sack after supper, . 2s. 6d.
  Item bread, . . 0½d.

Prince. O monstrous! but one half-pennyworth of bread to this intolerable deal of sack! What there is else keep close, we'll read it at more advantage: there let him sleep till day; I'll to the court in the morning. We must 530 all to the wars, and thy place shall be honourable. I'll procure this fat rogue a charge of foot, and I know his † death will be a march of twelve-score; the money shall be paid back again with advantage; be with me betimes in the morning, and so good morrow, Peto.

Peto. Good morrow, good my lord. *Exeunt*

Act Third

Bangor. The Archdeacon's house

Enter Hotspur, Worcester, Mortimer, and Glendower

Mortimer. These promises are fair, the parties sure,
  And our induction full of prosperous hope.
Hotspur. Lord Mortimer, and cousin Glendower,
  Will you sit down? And uncle Worcester:
  A plague upon it, I have forgot the map.
Glendower. No, here it is. Sit, cousin Percy, sit,
  Good cousin Hotspur, for by that name
  As oft as Lancaster doth speak of you,
  His cheek looks pale, and with a rising sigh
  He wisheth you in heaven.
Hotspur.   And you in hell,   10
  As oft as he hears Owen Glendower spoke of.
Glendower. I cannot blame him: at my nativity
  The front of heaven was full of fiery shapes,
  Of burning cressets, and at my birth
  The frame and huge foundation of the earth
  Shak'd like a coward.
Hotspur.   Why, so it would have done
  At the same season, if your mother's cat
  Had but kitten'd, though yourself had ne'er been born.
Glendower. I say the earth did shake when I was born.
Hotspur. And I say the earth was not of my mind,   20
  If you suppose as fearing you it shook.
Glendower. The heavens were all on fire, the earth did
    tremble.
Hotspur. O, then the earth shook to see the heavens on
    fire,

And not in fear of your nativity.
Diseased nature oftentimes breaks forth,
In strange eruptions; oft the teeming earth
Is with a kind of colic pinch'd and vex'd,
By the imprisoning of unruly wind
Within her womb, which, for enlargement striving,
Shakes the old beldam earth, and topples down   30
Steeples and moss-grown towers. At your birth
Our grandam earth, having this distemperature,
In passion shook.
Glendower.   Cousin, of many men
I do not bear these crossings; give me leave
To tell you once again that at my birth
The front of heaven was full of fiery shapes,
The goats ran from the mountains, and the herds
Were strangely clamorous to the frighted fields.
These signs have mark'd me extraordinary,
And all the courses of my life do show   40
I am not in the roll of common men.
Where is he living, clipp'd in with the sea
That chides the banks of England, Scotland, Wales,
Which calls me pupil, or hath read to me?
And bring him out that is but woman's son
Can trace me in the tedious ways of art,
And hold me pace in deep experiments.
Hotspur. I think there is no man speaks better Welsh.
I'll to dinner.
Mortimer. Peace, cousin Percy, you will make him mad.   50
Glendower. I can call spirits from the vasty deep.
Hotspur. Why, so can I, or so can any man,
But will they come when you do call for them?
Glendower. Why, I can teach you, cousin, to command   †
the devil.
Hotspur. And I can teach thee, coz, to shame the devil,
By telling truth. Tell truth, and shame the devil.
If thou have power to raise him, bring him hither,
And I'll be sworn I have power to shame him hence.

O, while you live, tell truth, and shame the devil!

Mortimer. Come, come, no more of this unprofitable chat.   60

Glendower. Three times hath Henry Bolingbroke made
   head
  Against my power, thrice from the banks of Wye
  And sandy-bottom'd Severn have I sent
  Him bootless home and weather-beaten back.

Hotspur. Home without boots, and in foul weather too!
  How 'scapes he agues, in the devil's name?

Glendower. Come, here's the map: shall we divide our
   right
  According to our threefold order ta'en?

Mortimer. The archdeacon hath divided it
  Into three limits very equally: 70
  England, from Trent, and Severn hitherto,
  By south and east is to my part assign'd:
  All westward, Wales beyond the Severn shore,
  And all the fertile land within that bound,
  To Owen Glendower: and, dear coz, to you
  The remnant northward, lying off from Trent.
  And our indentures tripartite are drawn;
  Which being sealed interchangeably,
  (A business that this night may execute,)
  To-morrow, cousin Percy, you and I   80
  And my good Lord of Worcester will set forth
  To meet your father and the Scottish power,
  As is appointed us, at Shrewsbury.
  My father Glendower is not ready yet,
  Nor shall we need his help these fourteen days.
  Within that space you may have drawn together
  Your tenants, friends, and neighbouring gentlemen.

Glendower. A shorter time shall send me to you, lords:
  And in my conduct shall your ladies come,
  From whom you now must steal and take no leave,   90
  For there will be a world of water shed
  Upon the parting of your wives and you.

Hotspur. Methinks my moiety, north from Burton here,

In quantity equals not one of yours:
See how this river comes me cranking in,
And cuts me from the best of all my land
A huge half-moon, a monstrous cantle out.
I'll have the current in this place damm'd up,
And here the smug and silver Trent shall run
In a new channel fair and evenly;   100
It shall not wind with such a deep indent,
To rob me of so rich a bottom here.

Glendower. Not wind? it shall, it must, you see it doth.

Mortimer. Yea, but
Mark how he bears his course, and runs me up
With like advantage on the other side,
Gelding the opposed continent as much
As on the other side it takes from you.

Worcester. Yea, but a little charge will trench him here,
And on this north side win this cape of land,   110
And then he runs straight and even.

Hotspur. I'll have it so: a little charge will do it.

Glendower. I'll not have it alter'd.

Hotspur.   Will not you?

Glendower. No, nor you shall not.

Hotspur.   Who shall say me nay?

Glendower. Why, that will I.

Hotspur. Let me not understand you, then; speak it in
Welsh.

Glendower. I can speak English, lord, as well as you;
For I was train'd up in the English court,
Where, being but young, I framed to the harp   120
Many an English ditty lovely well,
And gave the tongue a helpful ornament,
A virtue that was never seen in you.

Hotspur. Marry,
And I am glad of it with all my heart:
I had rather be a kitten and cry mew
Than one of these same metre ballad-mongers;
I had rather hear a brazen canstick turn'd,

48

Or a dry wheel grate on the axle-tree,
And that would set my teeth nothing on edge,   130
Nothing so much as mincing poetry:
'Tis like the forc'd gait of a shuffling nag.
Glendower. Come, you shall have Trent turn'd.
Hotspur. I do not care, I'll give thrice so much land
    To any well-deserving friend;
    But in the way of bargain, mark ye me,
    I'll cavil on the ninth part of a hair.
    Are the indentures drawn? shall we be gone?
Glendower. The moon shines fair; you may away by
        night:
    I'll haste the writer, and withal   140
    Break with your wives of your departure hence:
    I am afraid my daughter will run mad,
    So much she doteth on her Mortimer.   *Exit*
Mortimer. Fie, cousin Percy! how you cross my father!
Hotspur. I cannot choose: sometime he angers me
    With telling me of the moldwarp and the ant,
    Of the dreamer Merlin and his prophecies,
    And of a dragon and a finless fish,
    A clip-wing'd griffin and a moulten raven,
    A couching lion and a ramping cat,   150
    And such a deal of skimble-skamble stuff
    As puts me from my faith. I tell you what,—
    He held me last night at least nine hours
    In reckoning up the several devils' names
    That were his lackeys: I cried 'hum,' and 'well, go to,'
    But mark'd him not a word. O, he is as tedious
    As a tired horse, a railing wife,
    Worse than a smoky house: I had rather live
    With cheese and garlic in a windmill, far,
    Than feed on cates and have him talk to me   160
    In any summer-house in Christendom.
Mortimer. In faith, he is a worthy gentleman,
    Exceedingly well read, and profited
    In strange concealments, valiant as a lion,

And wondrous affable; and as bountiful
As mines of India. Shall I tell you, cousin?
He holds your temper in a high respect,
And curbs himself even of his natural scope
When you come 'cross his humour; faith, he does:
I warrant you, that man is not alive   170
Might so have tempted him as you have done,
Without the taste of danger and reproof:
But do not use it oft, let me entreat you.

Worcester. In faith, my lord, you are too wilful-blame,
And since your coming hither have done enough
To put him quite beside his patience;
You must needs learn, lord, to amend this fault:
Though sometimes it show greatness, courage, blood,—
And that's the dearest grace it renders you,—
Yet oftentimes it doth present harsh rage,   180
Defect of manners, want of government,
Pride, haughtiness, opinion, and disdain,
The least of which haunting a noble man
Loseth men's hearts, and leaves behind a stain
Upon the beauty of all parts besides,
Beguiling them of commendation.

Hotspur. Well, I am school'd: good manners be your
    speed!
Here come our wives, and let us take our leave.

Re-enter Glendower with the ladies

Mortimer. This is the deadly spite that angers me;
My wife can speak no English, I no Welsh.   190

Glendower. My daughter weeps: she'll not part with you;
She'll be a soldier too, she'll to the wars.

Mortimer. Good father, tell her that she and my aunt
    Percy
Shall follow in your conduct speedily.

> *Glendower speaks to her in Welsh, and she*
> *answers him in the same*

Glendower. She is desperate here; a peevish self-will'd †
  harlotry, one that no persuasion can do good upon.
                      The lady speaks in Welsh
Mortimer. I understand thy looks: that pretty Welsh
  Which thou pourest down from these swelling heavens
  I am too perfect in; and, but for shame,
  In such a parley should I answer thee.   200
              The lady speaks again in Welsh
  I understand thy kisses, and thou mine,
  And that's a feeling disputation:
  But I will never be a truant, love,
  Till I have learn'd thy language, for thy tongue
  Makes Welsh as sweet as ditties highly penn'd,
  Sung by a fair queen in a summer's bower,
  With ravishing division, to her lute.
Glendower. Nay, if you melt, then will she run mad.
              The lady speaks again in Welsh
Mortimer. O, I am ignorance itself in this!
Glendower. She bids you on the wanton rushes lay you
    down   210
  And rest your gentle head upon her lap,
  And she will sing the song that pleaseth you,
  And on your eyelids crown the god of sleep,
  Charming your blood with pleasing heaviness,
  Making such difference 'twixt wake and sleep
  As is the difference betwixt day and night,
  The hour before the heavenly-harness'd team
  Begins his golden progress in the east.
Mortimer. With all my heart I'll sit and hear her sing:
  By that time will our book, I think, be drawn.   220
Glendower. Do so;
  And those musicians that shall play to you
  Hang in the air a thousand leagues from hence,
  And straight they shall be here: sit, and attend.
Hotspur. Come, Kate, thou art perfect in lying down:
  Come quick, quick, that I may lay my head in thy lap.

51

Lady Percy. Go, ye giddy goose.   *The music plays*
Hotspur. Now I perceive the devil understands Welsh:
    And 'tis no marvel he is so humorous.
    By 'r lady, he is a good musician.   230
Lady Percy. Then should you be nothing but musical, for
    you are altogether governed by humours. Lie still, ye
    thief, and hear the lady sing in Welsh.
Hotspur. I had rather hear Lady, my brach, howl in Irish.
Lady Percy. Wouldst thou have thy head broken?
Hotspur. No.
Lady Percy. Then be still.
Hotspur. Neither, 'tis a woman's fault.
Lady Percy. Now God help thee!
Hotspur. To the Welsh lady's bed.   240
Lady Percy. What's that?
Hotspur. Peace! she sings.
         Here the lady sings a Welsh song
Hotspur. Come, Kate, I'll have your song too.
Lady Percy. Not mine, in good sooth.
Hotspur. Not yours, in good sooth! Heart! you swear like
    a comfit-maker's wife. 'Not you, in good sooth,' and
    'as true as I live,' and 'as God shall mend me,' and 'as
    sure as day,'
    And givest such sarcenet surety for thy oaths,
    As if thou never walk'st further than Finsbury.   250
    Swear me, Kate, like a lady as thou art,
    A good mouth-filling oath, and leave 'in sooth,'
    And such protest of pepper-gingerbread,
    To velvet-guards and Sunday-citizens.
    Come, sing.
Lady Percy. I will not sing.
Hotspur. 'Tis the next way to turn tailor, or be redbreast
    teacher. An the indentures be drawn, I'll away within
    these two hours, and so come in when ye will. *Exit*
Glendower. Come, come, Lord Mortimer; you are as
    slow   260

As hot Lord Percy is on fire to go.
By this our book is drawn, we'll but seal, and then
To horse immediately.
Mortimer.   With all my heart.   *Exeunt*

London. The palace

Enter the King, Prince of Wales, and others

King. Lords, give us leave; the Prince of Wales and I
    Must have some private conference, but be near at
        hand,
    For we shall presently have need of you.
                                        Exeunt Lords
    I know not whether God will have it so,
    For some displeasing service I have done,
    That, in his secret doom, out of my blood
    He'll breed revengement and a scourge for me;
    But thou dost in thy passages of life
    Make me believe that thou art only mark'd
    For the hot vengeance, and the rod of heaven,   10
    To punish my mistreadings. Tell me else,
    Could such inordinate and low desires,
    Such poor, such bare, such lewd, such mean attempts,
    Such barren pleasures, rude society,
    As thou art match'd withal, and grafted to,
    Accompany the greatness of thy blood,
    And hold their level with thy princely heart?
Prince. So please your majesty, I would I could
    Quit all offences with as clear excuse
    As well as I am doubtless I can purge   20
    Myself of many I am charg'd withal;
    Yet such extenuation let me beg,
    As, in reproof of many tales devis'd,
    Which oft the ear of greatness needs must hear,
    By smiling pick-thanks, and base newsmongers,

I may, for some things true, wherein my youth
Hath faulty wander'd, and irregular,
Find pardon on my true submission.
King. God pardon thee! yet let me wonder, Harry,
At thy affections, which do hold a wing   30
Quite from the flight of all thy ancestors.
Thy place in council thou hast rudely lost,
Which by thy younger brother is supplied,
And art almost an alien to the hearts
Of all the court and princes of my blood:
The hope and expectation of thy time
Is ruin'd, and the soul of every man
Prophetically do forethink thy fall.
Had I so lavish of my presence been,
So common-hackney'd in the eyes of men,   40
So stale and cheap to vulgar company,
Opinion, that did help me to the crown,
Had still kept loyal to possession,
And left me in reputeless banishment,
A fellow of no mark nor likelihood.
By being seldom seen, I could not stir
But like a comet I was wonder'd at;
That men would tell their children 'This is he;'
Others would say 'Where, which is Bolingbroke?'
And then I stole all courtesy from heaven,   50
And dress'd myself in such humility
That I did pluck allegiance from men's hearts,
Loud shouts and salutations from their mouths,
Even in the presence of the crowned king.
Thus did I keep my person fresh and new;
My presence like a robe pontifical,
Ne'er seen but wonder'd at, and so my state,
Seldom but sumptuous, showed like a feast,
And won by rareness such solemnity.
The skipping king, he ambled up and down,   60
With shallow jesters, and rash bavin wits,
Soon kindled, and soon burnt; carded his state,

54

Mingled his royalty with capering fools,
Had his great name profaned with their scorns,
And gave his countenance, against his name,
To laugh at gibing boys, and stand the push
Of every beardless vain comparative,
Grew a companion to the common streets,
Enfeoff'd himself to popularity,
That, being daily swallow'd by men's eyes,   70
They surfeited with honey, and began
To loathe the taste of sweetness, whereof a little
More than a little is by much too much.
So when he had occasion to be seen,
He was but as the cuckoo is in June,
Heard, not regarded; seen, but with such eyes
As, sick and blunted with community,
Afford no extraordinary gaze,
Such as is bent on sun-like majesty
When it shines seldom in admiring eyes,   80
But rather drowz'd, and hung their eyelids down,
Slept in his face, and render'd such aspect
As cloudy men use to their adversaries,
Being with his presence glutted, gorg'd, and full.
And in that very line, Harry, standest thou,
For thou hast lost thy princely privilege
With vile participation. Not an eye
But is a-weary of thy common sight,
Save mine, which hath desir'd to see thee more,
Which now doth that I would not have it do,   90
Make blind itself with foolish tenderness.
Prince. I shall hereafter, my thrice gracious lord,
  Be more myself.
King.   For all the world
  As thou art to this hour was Richard then,
  When I from France set foot at Ravenspurgh,
  And even as I was then, is Percy now.
  Now, by my sceptre, and my soul to boot,
  He hath more worthy interest to the state

Than thou the shadow of succession;
For of no right, nor colour like to right,   100
He doth fill fields with harness in the realm,
Turns head against the lion's armed jaws,
And, being no more in debt to years than thou,
Leads ancient lords and reverend bishops on
To bloody battles and to bruising arms.
What never-dying honour hath he got
Against renowned Douglas! whose high deeds,
Whose hot incursions, and great name in arms,
Holds from all soldiers chief majority
And military title capital   110
Through all the kingdoms that acknowledge Christ:
Thrice hath this Hotspur Mars in swathling clothes,
This infant warrior, in his enterprises
Discomfited great Douglas, ta'en him once,
Enlarged him, and made a friend of him,
To fill the mouth of deep defiance up,
And shake the peace and safety of our throne.
And what say you to this? Percy, Northumberland,
The Archbishop's grace of York, Douglas, Mortimer,
Capitulate against us, and are up.   120
But wherefore do I tell these news to thee?
Why, Harry, do I tell thee of my foes,
Which art my nearest and dearest enemy?
Thou that art like enough through vassal fear,
Base inclination, and the start of spleen,
To fight against me under Percy's pay,
To dog his heels, and curtsy at his frowns,
To show how much thou art degenerate.
Prince. Do not think so, you shall not find it so,
And God forgive them that so much have sway'd   130
Your majesty's good thoughts away from me!
I will redeem all this on Percy's head,
And in the closing of some glorious day
Be bold to tell you that I am your son,
When I will wear a garment all of blood,

And stain my favours in a bloody mask,
Which, wash'd away, shall scour my shame with it,
And that shall be the day, whene'er it lights,
That this same child of honour and renown,
This gallant Hotspur, this all-praised knight,   140
And your unthought-of Harry chance to meet.
For every honour sitting on his helm,
Would they were multitudes, and on my head
My shames redoubled! For the time will come
That I shall make this northern youth exchange
His glorious deeds for my indignities.
Percy is but my factor, good my lord,
To engross up glorious deeds on my behalf;
And I will call him to so strict account,
That he shall render every glory up,   150
Yea, even the slightest worship of his time,
Or I will tear the reckoning from his heart.
This in the name of God I promise here:
The which if He be pleased I shall perform,
I do beseech your majesty may salve
The long-grown wounds of my intemperance:
If not, the end of life cancels all bands,
And I will die a hundred thousand deaths
Ere break the smallest parcel of this vow.
King. A hundred thousand rebels die in this;   160
Thou shalt have charge and sovereign trust herein.

Enter Blunt

How now, good Blunt? thy looks are full of speed.
Blunt. So hath the business that I come to speak of.
Lord Mortimer of Scotland hath sent word
That Douglas and the English rebels met
The eleventh of this month at Shrewsbury;
A mighty and a fearful head they are,
If promises be kept on every hand,
As ever offer'd foul play in a state.
King. The Earl of Westmoreland set forth to-day,   170

With him my son, Lord John of Lancaster,
For this advertisement is five days old:
On Wednesday next, Harry, you shall set forward,
On Thursday we ourselves will march.
Our meeting is Bridgenorth, and, Harry, you
Shall march through Gloucestershire, by which ac-
count,
Our business valued, some twelve days hence
Our general forces at Bridgenorth shall meet.
Our hands are full of business, let's away;
Advantage feeds him fat while men delay.   *Exeunt*   180

SCENE III

The Boar's-Head Tavern in Eastcheap

Enter Falstaff and Bardolph

Falstaff. Bardolph, am I not fallen away vilely since this last action? do I not bate? do I not dwindle? Why, my skin hangs about me like an old lady's loose gown. I am withered like an old apple-john. Well, I'll repent, and that suddenly, while I am in some liking; I shall be out of heart shortly, and then I shall have no strength to repent. An I have not forgotten what the inside of a church is made of, I am a peppercorn, a brewer's horse: the inside of a church! Company, villanous company, hath been the spoil of me.   10

Bardolph. Sir John, you are so fretful, you cannot live long.

Falstaff. Why, there is it: come sing me a bawdy song, make me merry. I was as virtuously given as a gentleman need to be, virtuous enough, swore little, dic'd not above seven times a week, went to a bawdy-house not above once in a quarter of an hour, paid money that I borrowed three or four times, lived well, and in good compass, and now I live out of all order, out of all compass.   20

Bardolph. Why, you are so fat, Sir John, that you must
needs be out of all compass; out of all reasonable
compass, Sir John.

Falstaff. Do thou amend thy face, and I'll amend my life:
thou art our admiral, thou bearest the lantern in the
poop, but 'tis in the nose of thee; thou art the Knight
of the Burning Lamp.

Bardolph. Why, Sir John, my face does you no harm.

Falstaff. No, I'll be sworn, I make as good use of it as
many a man doth of a Death's-head, or a *memento*   30
mori. I never see thy face but I think upon hell-fire,
and Dives that lived in purple: for there he is in his
robes, burning, burning. If thou wert any way given to
virtue, I would swear by thy face; my oath should be,
'By this fire, that's God's angel.' But thou art altogether
given over; and wert indeed, but for the light in thy
face, the son of utter darkness. When thou ran'st up
Gadshill in the night to catch my horse, if I did not
think thou hadst been an *ignis fatuus,* or a ball of wildfire, there's no purchase in money. O, thou art a per-   40
petual triumph, an everlasting bonfire-light, thou hast
saved me a thousand marks in links and torches, walk-
ing with thee in the night betwixt tavern and tavern;
but the sack that thou hast drunk me, would have
bought me lights as good cheap, at the dearest chan-
dler's in Europe. I have maintained that salamander of
yours with fire any time this two and thirty years, God
reward me for it!

Bardolph. 'Sblood, I would my face were in your belly!

Falstaff. God-a-mercy, so should I be sure to be heart-   50
burn'd!

Enter Mistress Quickly

How now, Dame Partlet the hen, have you inquir'd
yet who pick'd my pocket?

Quickly. Why, Sir John, what do you think, Sir John? do
you think I keep thieves in my house? I have search'd,

I have inquir'd, so has my husband, man by man, boy
by boy, servant by servant; the tithe of a hair was   †
never lost in my house before.

Falstaff. Ye lie, hostess: Bardolph was shav'd, and lost
many a hair, and I'll be sworn my pocket was pick'd: 60
go to, you are a woman, go.

Quickly. Who, I? no; I defy thee: God's light, I was never
call'd so in mine own house before.

Falstaff. Go to, I know you well enough.

Quickly. No, Sir John, you do not know me, Sir John, I
know you, Sir John, you owe me money, Sir John, and
now you pick a quarrel to beguile me of it, I bought
you a dozen of shirts to your back.

Falstaff. Dowlas, filthy dowlas: I have given them away
to bakers' wives, they have made bolters of them.   70

Quickly. Now, as I am a true woman, holland of eight
shillings an ell, you owe money here besides, Sir John,
for your diet, and by-drinkings, and money lent you,
four and twenty pound.

Falstaff. He had his part of it, let him pay.

Quickly. He? alas, he is poor, he hath nothing.

Falstaff. How? poor? look upon his face. What call you
rich? let them coin his nose, let them coin his cheeks,
I'll not pay a denier. What, will you make a younker
of me? shall I not take mine ease in mine inn, but I   80
shall have my pocket pick'd? I have lost a seal-ring of
my grandfather's worth forty mark.

Quickly. O Jesu, I have heard the prince tell him, I know
not how oft, that that ring was copper!

Falstaff. How? the prince is a Jack, a sneak-cup: 'sblood,
an he were here, I would cudgel him like a dog, if he
would say so.

*Enter the Prince and Peto, marching, and Falstaff meets them
playing on his truncheon like a fife*

How now, lad? is the wind in that door, i' faith? must
we all march?

Bardolph. Yea, two and two, Newgate fashion.   90

Quickly. My lord, I pray you, hear me.

Prince. What sayest thou, Mistress Quickly? How doth thy husband? I love him well, he is an honest man.

Quickly. Good my lord, hear me.

Falstaff. Prithee let her alone, and list to me.

Prince. What say'st thou, Jack?

Falstaff. The other night I fell asleep here, behind the arras, and had my pocket pick'd; this house is turn'd bawdy-house, they pick pockets.

Prince. What didst thou lose, Jack?   100

Falstaff. Wilt thou believe me, Hal, three or four bonds of forty pound a-piece, and a seal-ring of my grandfather's.

Prince. A trifle, some eight-penny matter.

Quickly. So I told him, my lord, and I said I heard your grace say so: and, my lord, he speaks most vilely of you, like a foul-mouth'd man as he is, and said he would cudgel you.

Prince. What! he did not?

Quickly. There's neither faith, truth, nor womanhood in   110 me else.

Falstaff. There's no more faith in thee than in a stew'd prune, nor no more truth in thee than in a drawn fox, and for womanhood, Maid Marian may be the deputy's wife of the ward to thee. Go, you thing, go.

Quickly. Say, what thing? what thing?

Falstaff. What thing? why, a thing to thank God on.

Quickly. I am no thing to thank God on, I would thou shouldst know it, I am an honest man's wife, and, setting thy knighthood aside, thou art a knave to call me   120 so.

Falstaff. Setting thy womanhood aside, thou art a beast to say otherwise.

Quickly. Say, what beast, thou knave, thou?

Falstaff. What beast? why, an otter.

Prince. An otter, Sir John, why an otter?

Falstaff. Why? she's neither fish nor flesh, a man knows
not where to have her.

Quickly. Thou art an unjust man in saying so, thou or
any man knows where to have me, thou knave, thou!   130

Prince. Thou sayst true, hostess, and he slanders thee
most grossly.

Quickly. So he doth you, my lord, and said this other day
you ought him a thousand pound.

Prince. Sirrah, do I owe you a thousand pound?

Falstaff. A thousand pound, Hal? a million, thy love is
worth a million, thou owest me thy love.

Quickly. Nay, my lord, he called you Jack, and said he
would cudgel you.

Falstaff. Did I, Bardolph?   140

Bardolph. Indeed, Sir John, you said so.

Falstaff. Yea, if he said my ring was copper.

Prince. I say 'tis copper, darest thou be as good as thy
word now?

Falstaff. Why, Hal! Thou knowest as thou art but man I
dare, but as thou art prince, I fear thee as I fear the
roaring of the lion's whelp.

Prince. And why not as the lion?

Falstaff. The king himself is to be feared as the lion; dost
thou think I'll fear thee as I fear thy father? nay, an I   150
do, I pray God my girdle break.

Prince. O, if it should, how would thy guts fall about thy
knees! But, sirrah, there's no room for faith, truth, nor
honesty in this bosom of thine; it is all fill'd up with
guts, and midriff. Charge an honest woman with picking thy pocket! why, thou whoreson, impudent, emboss'd rascal, if there were anything in thy pocket but
tavern-reckonings, memorandums of bawdy-houses,
and one poor penny-worth of sugar-candy to make thee
long-winded, if thy pocket were enrich'd with any other   160
injuries but these, I am a villain: and yet you will stand
to it, you will not pocket up wrong; art thou not
ashamed?

Falstaff. Dost thou hear, Hal? thou knowest in the state
of innocency Adam fell, and what should poor Jack
Falstaff do in the days of villany? Thou seest I have
more flesh than another man, and therefore more
frailty. You confess then, you pick'd my pocket?

Prince. It appears so by the story.

Falstaff. Hostess, I forgive thee, go, make ready break-   170
fast, love thy husband, look to thy servants, cherish thy
guests, thou shalt find me tractable to any honest reason, thou seest I am pacified still. Nay, prithee be gone.
(*exit Mistress Quickly*.) Now, Hal, to the news at
court; for the robbery, lad, how is that answered?

Prince. O, my sweet beef, I must still be good angel to
thee; the money is paid back again.

Falstaff. O, I do not like that paying back, 'tis a double
labour.

Prince. I am good friends with my father, and may do any   180
thing.

Falstaff. Rob me the exchequer the first thing thou doest,
and do it with unwash'd hands too.

Bardolph. Do, my lord.

Prince. I have procured thee, Jack, a charge of foot.

Falstaff. I would it had been of horse. Where shall I find
one that can steal well? O for a fine thief, of the age
of two and twenty or thereabouts! I am heinously un-
provided. Well, God be thanked for these rebels, they
offend none but the virtuous; I laud them, I praise   190
them.

Prince. Bardolph!

Bardolph. My lord?

Prince. Go bear this letter to Lord John of Lancaster,   †
To my brother John; this to my Lord of Westmoreland.
Exit Bardolph
Go, Peto, to horse, to horse, for thou and I
Have thirty miles to ride yet ere dinner time.
Exit Peto

63

Jack, meet me to-morrow in the Temple hall
At two o'clock in the afternoon.
There shalt thou know thy charge, and there receive   200
Money and order for their furniture.
The land is burning; Percy stands on high;
And either we or they must lower lie.   *Exit*
Falstaff. Rare words! brave world! Hostess, my breakfast,
    come!
    O, I could wish this tavern were my drum!   *Exit*

Act Fourth

SCENE I

The rebel camp near Shrewsbury

Enter Hotspur, Worcester, and Douglas

Hotspur. Well said, my noble Scot: if speaking truth
    In this fine age were not thought flattery,
    Such attribution should the Douglas have,
    As not a soldier of this season's stamp
    Should go so general current through the world.
    By God, I cannot flatter, I do defy
    The tongues of soothers, but a braver place
    In my heart's love hath no man than yourself:
    Nay, task me to my word, approve me, lord.
Douglas. Thou art the king of honour: 10
    No man so potent breathes upon the ground
    But I will beard him.
Hotspur.   Do so, and 'tis well.

Enter a Messenger with letters

What letters hast thou there?—I can but thank you.

64

Messenger. These letters come from your father.

Hotspur. Letters from him? why comes he not himself?

Messenger. He cannot come, my lord, he is grievous sick.

Hotspur. 'Zounds, how has he the leisure to be sick   †
  In such a justling time? Who leads his power?
  Under whose government come they along?

Messenger. His letters bear his mind, not I, my lord.   20

Worcester. I prithee tell me, doth he keep his bed?

Messenger. He did, my lord, four days ere I set forth,
  And at the time of my departure thence
  He was much fear'd by his physicians.

Worcester. I would the state of time had first been whole,
  Ere he by sickness had been visited;
  His health was never better worth than now.

Hotspur. Sick now! droop now! this sickness doth infect
  The very life-blood of our enterprise;
  'Tis catching hither, even to our camp;   30
  He writes me here, that inward sickness—
  And that his friends by deputation could not
  So soon be drawn, nor did he think it meet
  To lay so dangerous and dear a trust
  On any soul remov'd but on his own—
  Yet doth he give us bold advertisement,
  That with our small conjunction we should on,
  To see how fortune is dispos'd to us,
  For, as he writes, there is no quailing now,
  Because the king is certainly possess'd   40
  Of all our purposes. What say you to it?

Worcester. Your father's sickness is a maim to us.

Hotspur. A perilous gash, a very limb lopp'd off:
  And yet, in faith, it is not; his present want
  Seems more than we shall find it: were it good
  To set the exact wealth of all our states
  All at one cast? to set so rich a main
  On the nice hazard of one doubtful hour?
  It were not good; for therein should we read

The very bottom and the soul of hope,   50
The very list, the very utmost bound
Of all our fortunes.

Douglas.   Faith, and so we should;
Where now remains a sweet reversion:
We may boldly spend upon the hope of what
Is to come in:
A comfort of retirement lives in this.

Hotspur. A rendezvous, a home to fly unto,
If that the devil and mischance look big
Upon the maidenhead of our affairs.

Worcester. But yet I would your father had been here.   60
The quality and hair of our attempt
Brooks no division, it will be thought
By some, that know not why he is away,
That wisdom, loyalty and mere dislike
Of our proceedings kept the earl from hence:
And think how such an apprehension
May turn the tide of fearful faction,
And breed a kind of question in our cause;
For well you know we of the offering side
Must keep aloof from strict arbitrement,   70
And stop all sight-holes, every loop, from whence
The eye of reason may pry in upon us:
This absence of your father's draws a curtain,
That shows the ignorant a kind of fear
Before not dreamt of.

Hotspur.   You strain too far.
I rather of his absence make this use,
It lends a lustre and more great opinion,
A larger dare to our great enterprise,
Than if the earl were here, for men must think,
If we without his help can make a head   80
To push against a kingdom, with his help
We shall o'erturn it topsy-turvy down;
Yet all goes well, yet all our joints are whole.

Douglas. As heart can think; there is not such a word
  Spoke of in Scotland as this term of fear.

Enter Sir Richard Vernon

Hotspur. My cousin Vernon, welcome, by my soul!
Vernon. Pray God my news be worth a welcome, lord.
  The Earl of Westmoreland, seven thousand strong,
  Is marching hitherwards, with him Prince John.
Hotspur. No harm; what more?
Vernon.   And further, I have learn'd,   90
  The king himself in person is set forth,
  Or hitherwards intended speedily,
  With strong and mighty preparation.
Hotspur. He shall be welcome too. Where is his son,
  The nimble-footed madcap Prince of Wales,
  And his comrades, that daff'd the world aside,
  And bid it pass?
Vernon.   All furnish'd, all in arms;
  All plum'd like estridges that with the wind   †
  Baited like eagles having lately bath'd,
  Glittering in golden coats, like images,   100
  As full of spirit as the month of May,
  And gorgeous as the sun at midsummer;
  Wanton as youthful goats, wild as young bulls.
  I saw young Harry, with his beaver on,
  His cuisses on his thighs, gallantly arm'd,
  Rise from the ground like feather'd Mercury,
  And vaulted with such ease into his seat,
  As if an angel dropp'd down from the clouds,
  To turn and wind a fiery Pegasus,
  And witch the world with noble horsemanship.   110
Hotspur. No more, no more: worse than the sun in
  March,
  This praise doth nourish agues. Let them come;
  They come like sacrifices in their trim,
  And to the fire-ey'd maid of smoky war
  All hot and bleeding will we offer them:

The mailed Mars shall on his altars sit
Up to the ears in blood. I am on fire
To hear this rich reprisal is so nigh
And yet not ours. Come, let me taste my horse,
Who is to bear me like a thunderbolt   120
Against the bosom of the Prince of Wales:
Harry to Harry shall, hot horse to horse,
Meet and ne'er part till one drop down a corse.
O that Glendower were come!
Vernon.   There is more news:
I learn'd in Worcester, as I rode along,
He cannot draw his power this fourteen days.
Douglas. That's the worst tidings that I hear of yet.
Worcester. Ay, by my faith, that bears a frosty sound.
Hotspur. What may the king's whole battle reach unto?
Vernon. To thirty thousand.
Hotspur.   Forty let it be: 130
My father and Glendower being both away,
The powers of us may serve so great a day.
Come, let us take a muster speedily:
Doomsday is near; die all, die merrily.
Douglas. Talk not of dying; I am out of fear
Of death or death's hand for this one half year.

                                        Exeunt

SCENE II

A public road near Coventry

Enter Falstaff and Bardolph

Falstaff. Bardolph, get thee before to Coventry, fill me a
bottle of sack, our soldiers shall march through; we'll
to Sutton Cop-hill to-night.   †
Bardolph. Will you give me money, captain?
Falstaff. Lay out, lay out.
Bardolph. This bottle makes an angel.
Falstaff. An if it do, take it for thy labour, an if it make

68

twenty, take them all; I'll answer the coinage. Bid my
lieutenant Peto meet me at town's end.

Bardolph. I will, captain: farewell.   *Exit*   10

Falstaff. If I be not ashamed of my soldiers, I am a sous'd
gurnet; I have misused the king's press damnably. I
have got in exchange of a hundred and fifty soldiers
three hundred and odd pounds. I press me none but
good householders, yeomen's sons, inquire me out con-
tracted bachelors, such as had been asked twice on the
banns, such a commodity of warm slaves, as had as
lieve hear the devil as a drum, such as fear the report
of a caliver worse than a struck fowl, or a hurt wild-
duck. I press'd me none but such toasts-and-butter,   20
with hearts in their bellies no bigger than pins'-heads,
and they have bought out their services, and now my
whole charge consists of ancients, corporals, lieuten-
ants, gentlemen of companies; slaves as ragged as
Lazarus in the painted cloth, where the glutton's dogs
licked his sores, and such as indeed were never soldiers, but discarded unjust serving-men, younger sons
to younger brothers, revolted tapsters, and ostlers,
trade-fallen, the cankers of a calm world and a long
peace, ten times more dishonourable ragged than an   30
old fac'd ancient, and such have I to fill up the rooms
of them that have bought out their services, that you
would think that I had a hundred and fifty tattered
prodigals, lately come from swine-keeping, from eating
draff and husks. A mad fellow met me on the way, and
told me I had unloaded all the gibbets, and press'd the
dead bodies. No eye hath seen such scarecrows. I'll not
march through Coventry with them, that's flat: nay,
and the villains march wide betwixt the legs, as if they
had gyves on, for indeed I had the most of them out of   40
prison; there's not a shirt and a half in all my company,   †
and the half shirt is two napkins tack'd together, and
thrown over the shoulders like a herald's coat without
sleeves, and the shirt, to say the truth, stolen from my

69

host at Saint Alban's, or the red-nose innkeeper of
Daventry, but that's all one, they'll find linen enough
on every hedge.

Enter the Prince and Westmoreland

Prince. How now, blown Jack? how now, quilt?

Falstaff. What, Hal, how now, mad wag? what a devil
dost thou in Warwickshire? My good Lord of West-   50
moreland, I cry you mercy, I thought your honour had
already been at Shrewsbury.

Westmoreland. Faith, Sir John, 'tis more than time that I
were there, and you too, but my powers are there already; the king, I can tell you, looks for us all, we must
away all night.

Falstaff. Tut, never fear me, I am as vigilant as a cat to
steal cream.

Prince. I think, to steal cream indeed, for thy theft hath
already made thee butter; but tell me, Jack, whose fel-   60
lows are these that come after?

Falstaff. Mine, Hal, mine.

Prince. I did never see such pitiful rascals.

Falstaff. Tut, tut, good enough to toss, food for powder,
food for powder, they'll fill a pit as well as better: tush,
man, mortal men, mortal men.

Westmoreland. Ay, but, Sir John, methinks they are ex-
ceeding poor and bare, too beggarly.

Falstaff. Faith, for their poverty, I know not where they
had that, and for their bareness, I am sure they never   70
learn'd that of me.

Prince. No, I'll be sworn, unless you call three fingers on
the ribs bare; but, sirrah, make haste, Percy is already
in the field.   *Exit*

Falstaff. What, is the king encamp'd?

Westmoreland. He is, Sir John, I fear we shall stay too
long.

Falstaff. Well,

To the latter end of a fray, and the beginning of a feast,
Fits a dull fighter and a keen guest.   *Exeunt*   80

The rebel camp near Shrewsbury

Enter Hotspur, Worcester, Douglas, and Vernon

Hotspur. We'll fight with him to-night.
Worcester.   It may not be.
Douglas. You give him then advantage.   †
Vernon.   Not a whit.
Hotspur. Why say you so? looks he not for supply?
Vernon. So do we.
Hotspur.   His is certain, ours is doubtful.
Worcester. Good cousin, be advis'd, stir not to-night.
Vernon. Do not, my lord.
Douglas.   You do not counsel well,
    You speak it out of fear, and cold heart.
Vernon. Do me no slander, Douglas; by my life,
    And I dare well maintain it with my life,
    If well-respected honour bid me on,   10
    I hold as little counsel with weak fear
    As you, my lord, or any Scot that this day lives: †
    Let it be seen to-morrow in the battle
    Which of us fears.
Douglas.   Yea, or to-night.
Vernon.   Content.
Hotspur. To-night, say I.
Vernon. Come, come, it may not be. I wonder much,
    Being men of such great leading as you are,
    That you foresee not what impediments
    Drag back our expedition: certain horse
    Of my cousin Vernon's are not yet come up: 20
    Your uncle Worcester's horse came but to-day,
    And now their pride and mettle is asleep,
    Their courage with hard labour tame and dull,

That not a horse is half the half of himself.
Hotspur. So are the horses of the enemy.
   In general journey bated and brought low;
   The better part of ours are full of rest.
Worcester. The number of the king exceedeth ours;
   For God's sake, cousin, stay till all come in.

                    The trumpet sounds a parley

                 Enter Sir Walter Blunt

Blunt. I come with gracious offers from the king,   30
   If you vouchsafe me hearing and respect.
Hotspur. Welcome, Sir Walter Blunt; and would to God
   You were of our determination!
   Some of us love you well, and even those some
   Envy your great deservings and good name,
   Because you are not of our quality,
   But stand against us like an enemy.
Blunt. And God defend but still I should stand so,
   So long as out of limit and true rule
   You stand against anointed majesty.   40
   But to my charge. The king hath sent to know
   The nature of your griefs, and whereupon
   You conjure from the breast of civil peace
   Such bold hostility, teaching his duteous land
   Audacious cruelty. If that the king
   Have any way your good deserts forgot,
   Which he confesseth to be manifold,
   He bids you name your griefs, and with all speed
   You shall have your desires with interest,
   And pardon absolute for yourself, and these   50
   Herein misled by your suggestion.
Hotspur. The king is kind, and well we know the king
   Knows at what time to promise, when to pay.
   My father, and my uncle, and myself
   Did give him that same royalty he wears,
   And when he was not six and twenty strong,
   Sick in the world's regard, wretched and low,

                        72

A poor unminded outlaw sneaking home,
My father gave him welcome to the shore,
And when he heard him swear and vow to God   60
He came but to be Duke of Lancaster,
To sue his livery, and beg his peace,
With tears of innocency, and terms of zeal,
My father, in kind heart and pity mov'd,
Swore him assistance, and perform'd it too.
Now when the lords and barons of the realm
Perceiv'd Northumberland did lean to him,
The more and less came in with cap and knee,
Met him in boroughs, cities, villages,
Attended him on bridges, stood in lanes,   70
Laid gifts before him, proffer'd him their oaths,
Gave him their heirs, as pages follow'd him,
Even at the heels, in golden multitudes.
He presently, as greatness knows itself,
Steps me a little higher than his vow
Made to my father while his blood was poor,
Upon the naked shore at Ravenspurgh,
And now forsooth takes on him to reform
Some certain edicts, and some strait decrees,
That lie too heavy on the commonwealth,   80
Cries out upon abuses, seems to weep
Over his country's wrongs, and by this face,
This seeming brow of justice, did he win
The hearts of all that he did angle for:
Proceeded further, cut me off the heads
Of all the favourites that the absent king
In deputation left behind him here,
When he was personal in the Irish war.
Blunt. Tut, I came not to hear this.
Hotspur.   Then to the point.
In short time after he depos'd the king,   90
Soon after that, depriv'd him of his life,
And in the neck of that, task'd the whole state,
To make that worse, suffer'd his kinsman March,

73

(Who is, if every owner were well plac'd,
Indeed his king), to be engag'd in Wales,
There without ransom to lie forfeited,
Disgrac'd me in my happy victories,
Sought to entrap me by intelligence,
Rated mine uncle from the council-board,
In rage dismiss'd my father from the court,   100
Broke oath on oath, committed wrong on wrong,
And in conclusion drove us to seek out
This head of safety, and withal to pry
Into his title, the which we find
Too indirect for long continuance.
Blunt. Shall I return this answer to the king?
Hotspur. Not so, Sir Walter: we'll withdraw a while.
Go to the king, and let there be impawn'd
Some surety for a safe return again,
And in the morning early shall mine uncle   110
Bring him our purposes, and so farewell.
Blunt. I would you would accept of grace and love.
Hotspur. And may be so we shall.
Blunt.   Pray God you do.

Exeunt

SCENE IV

York. The Archbishop's palace

Enter the Archbishop of York and Sir Michael

Archbishop. Hie, good Sir Michael, bear this sealed brief
With winged haste to the lord marshal,
This to my cousin Scroop, and all the rest
To whom they are directed. If you knew
How much they do import, you would make haste.
Michael. My good lord,
I guess their tenour.
Archbishop.   Like enough you do.
To-morrow, good Sir Michael, is a day

74

Wherein the fortune of ten thousand men
Must bide the touch; for, sir, at Shrewsbury,   10
As I am truly given to understand,
The king with mighty and quick-raised power
Meets with Lord Harry: and, I fear, Sir Michael,
What with the sickness of Northumberland,
Whose power was in the first proportion,
And what with Owen Glendower's absence thence,
Who with them was a rated sinew too,
And comes not in, o'er-ruled by prophecies,
I fear the power of Percy is too weak
To wage an instant trial with the king.   20
Michael. Why, my good lord, you need not fear;
There is Douglas, and Lord Mortimer.
Archbishop. No, Mortimer is not there.
Michael. But there is Mordake, Vernon, Lord Harry
    Percy,
And there is my Lord of Worcester, and a head
Of gallant warriors, noble gentlemen.
Archbishop. And so there is: but yet the king hath drawn
The special head of all the land together,
The Prince of Wales, Lord John of Lancaster,
The noble Westmoreland and warlike Blunt,   30
And many moe corivals and dear men
Of estimation and command in arms.
Michael. Doubt not, my lord, they shall be well oppos'd.
Archbishop. I hope no less, yet needful 'tis to fear;
And, to prevent the worst, Sir Michael, speed:
For if Lord Percy thrive not, ere the king
Dismiss his power, he means to visit us,
For he hath heard of our confederacy,
And 'tis but wisdom to make strong against him:
Therefore make haste; I must go write again   40
To other friends, and so farewell, Sir Michael.   *Exeunt*

75

Act Fifth

The King's camp near Shrewsbury

*Enter the King, the Prince of Wales, Lord John of Lancaster,
Sir Walter Blunt, and Falstaff*

King. How bloodily the sun begins to peer
    Above yon busky hill! the day looks pale
    At his distemperature.
Prince.   The southern wind
    Doth play the trumpet to his purposes,
    And by his hollow whistling in the leaves
    Foretells a tempest and a blustering day.
King. Then with the losers let it sympathise,
    For nothing can seem foul to those that win.
                    The trumpet sounds

Enter Worcester and Vernon

    How now, my Lord of Worcester? 'tis not well
    That you and I should meet upon such terms   10
    As now we meet. You have deceiv'd our trust,
    And made us doff our easy robes of peace,
    To crush our old limbs in ungentle steel:
    This is not well, my lord, this is not well.
    What say you to it? will you again unknit
    This churlish knot of all-abhorred war?
    And move in that obedient orb again
    Where you did give a fair and natural light,
    And be no more an exhal'd meteor,
    A prodigy of fear, and a portent   20
    Of broached mischief to the unborn times?

Worcester. Hear me, my liege:
  For mine own part, I could be well content
  To entertain the lag-end of my life
  With quiet hours; for, I protest,
  I have not sought the day of this dislike.
King. You have not sought it? how comes it, then?
Falstaff. Rebellion lay in his way, and he found it.
Prince. Peace, chewet, peace!
Worcester. It pleas'd your majesty to turn your looks   30
  Of favour from myself, and all our house;
  And yet I must remember you, my lord,
  We were the first and dearest of your friends.
  For you my staff of office did I break
  In Richard's time, and posted day and night
  To meet you on the way, and kiss your hand,
  When yet you were in place, and in account,
  Nothing so strong and fortunate as I.
  It was myself, my brother, and his son,
  That brought you home, and boldly did outdare   40
  The dangers of the time. You swore to us,
  And you did swear that oath at Doncaster,
  That you did nothing purpose 'gainst the state,
  Nor claim no further than your new-fall'n right,
  The seat of Gaunt, dukedom of Lancaster:
  To this we swore our aid. But in short space
  It rain'd down fortune showering on your head,
  And such a flood of greatness fell on you,
  What with our help, what with the absent king,
  What with the injuries of a wanton time,   50
  The seeming sufferances that you had borne,
  And the contrarious winds that held the king
  So long in his unlucky Irish wars,
  That all in England did repute him dead:
  And from this swarm of fair advantages
  You took occasion to be quickly woo'd
  To gripe the general sway into your hand,
  Forgot your oath to us at Doncaster,

77

And being fed by us you us'd us so
As that ungentle gull, the cuckoo's bird,   60
Useth the sparrow, did oppress our nest,
Grew by our feeding to so great a bulk
That even our love durst not come near your sight,
For fear of swallowing; but with nimble wing
We were enforc'd, for safety sake, to fly
Out of your sight, and raise this present head,
Whereby we stand opposed by such means
As you yourself have forg'd against yourself,
By unkind usage, dangerous countenance,
And violation of all faith and troth,   70
Sworn to us in your younger enterprise.

King. These things indeed you have articulate,
Proclaim'd at market crosses, read in churches,
To face the garment of rebellion
With some fine colour that may please the eye
Of fickle changelings and poor discontents,
Which gape and rub the elbow at the news
Of hurlyburly innovation;
And never yet did insurrection want
Such water-colours to impaint his cause,   80
Nor moody beggars, starving for a time
Of pellmell havoc and confusion.

Prince. In both your armies there is many a soul
Shall pay full dearly for this encounter,
If once they join in trial. Tell your nephew,
The Prince of Wales doth join with all the world
In praise of Henry Percy: by my hopes,
This present enterprise set off his head,
I do not think a braver gentleman,
More active, valiant, or more valiant young,   90
More daring, or more bold, is now alive
To grace this latter age with noble deeds.
For my part, I may speak it to my shame,
I have a truant been to chivalry,
And so I hear he doth account me too;

Yet this before my father's majesty—
I am content that he shall take the odds
Of his great name and estimation,
And will, to save the blood on either side,
Try fortune with him in a single fight.   100
King. And, Prince of Wales, so dare we venture thee,
Albeit considerations infinite
Do make against it. No, good Worcester, no,
We love our people well, even those we love
That are misled upon your cousin's part,
And, will they take the offer of our grace,
Both he, and they, and you, yea, every man
Shall be my friend again, and I'll be his:
So tell your cousin, and bring me word
What he will do. But if he will not yield,   110
Rebuke and dread correction wait on us,
And they shall do their office. So, be gone;
We will not now be troubled with reply:
We offer fair; take it advisedly.
                    Exeunt Worcester and Vernon
Prince. It will not be accepted, on my life;
The Douglas and the Hotspur both together
Are confident against the world in arms.
King. Hence, therefore, every leader to his charge,
For on their answer will we set on them,
And God befriend us as our cause is just!   120
              Exeunt all but the Prince of Wales and Falstaff
Falstaff. Hal, if thou see me down in the battle, and be-
stride me, so, 'tis a point of friendship.
Prince. Nothing but a colossus can do thee that friend-
ship. Say thy prayers, and farewell.
Falstaff. I would 'twere bed-time, Hal, and all well.
Prince. Why, thou owest God a death.   *Exit*
Falstaff. 'Tis not due yet, I would be loath to pay him before his day, what need I be so forward with him that
calls not on me? Well, 'tis no matter, honour pricks
me on, yea, but how if honour prick me off when I   130

79

come on? How then? can honour set to a leg? no: or an arm? no: or take away the grief of a wound? no. Honour hath no skill in surgery, then? no. What is honour? a word; what is in that word honour? what is that honour? air. A trim reckoning! Who hath it? he that died o' Wednesday. Doth he feel it? no. Doth he hear it? no. 'Tis insensible, then? yea, to the dead. But will it not live with the living? no. Why? detraction will not suffer it, therefore I'll none of it, honour is a mere scutcheon, and so ends my catechism. *Exit* 140

SCENE II

The rebel camp

Enter Worcester and Vernon

Worcester. O, no, my nephew must not know, Sir
    Richard,
  The liberal and kind offer of the king.
Vernon. 'Twere best he did.
Worcester.   Then are we all undone.
  It is not possible, it cannot be,
  The king should keep his word in loving us;
  He will suspect us still, and find a time
  To punish this offence in other faults:
  Suspicion all our lives shall be stuck full of eyes,
  For treason is but trusted like the fox,
  Who, ne'er so tame, so cherish'd and lock'd up,   10
  Will have a wild trick of his ancestors.
  Look how we can, or sad or merrily,
  Interpretation will misquote our looks,
  And we shall feed like oxen at a stall,
  The better cherish'd still the nearer death;
  My nephew's trespass may be well forgot,
  It hath the excuse of youth and heat of blood,
  And an adopted name of privilege,
  A hare-brain'd Hotspur govern'd by a spleen;

All his offences live upon my head   20
  And on his father's; we did train him on,
  And, his corruption being ta'en from us,
  We, as the spring of all, shall pay for all.
  Therefore, good cousin, let not Harry know,
  In any case, the offer of the king.
Vernon. Deliver what you will, I'll say 'tis so.
  Here comes your cousin.

Enter Hotspur and Douglas

Hotspur. My uncle is return'd;
  Deliver up my Lord of Westmoreland,
  Uncle, what news?   30
Worcester. The king will bid you battle presently.
Douglas. Defy him by the Lord of Westmoreland.
Hotspur. Lord Douglas, go you and tell him so.
Douglas. Marry, and shall, and very willingly.   *Exit*
Worcester. There is no seeming mercy in the king.
Hotspur. Did you beg any? God forbid!
Worcester. I told him gently of our grievances,
  Of his oath-breaking, which he mended thus,
  By now forswearing that he is forsworn:
  He calls us rebels, traitors, and will scourge   40
  With haughty arms this hateful name in us.

Re-enter Douglas

Douglas. Arm, gentlemen, to arms! for I have thrown
  A brave defiance in King Henry's teeth,
  And Westmoreland, that was engag'd, did bear it,
  Which cannot choose but bring him quickly on.
Worcester. The Prince of Wales stepp'd forth before the
    king,
  And, nephew, challeng'd you to single fight.
Hotspur. O, would the quarrel lay upon our heads,
  And that no man might draw short breath to-day
  But I and Harry Monmouth! Tell me, tell me,   50
  How show'd his tasking? seem'd it in contempt?

81

Vernon. No, by my soul, I never in my life
　Did hear a challenge urg'd more modestly,
　Unless a brother should a brother dare
　To gentle exercise and proof of arms.
　He gave you all the duties of a man,
　Trimm'd up your praises with a princely tongue,
　Spoke your deservings like a chronicle,
　Making you ever better than his praise
　By still dispraising praise valued with you,　　　　　60
　And, which became him like a prince indeed,
　He made a blushing cital of himself,
　And chid his truant youth with such a grace
　As if he master'd there a double spirit
　Of teaching and of learning instantly.
　There did he pause; but let me tell the world,
　If he outlive the envy of this day,
　England did never owe so sweet a hope,
　So much misconstrued in his wantonness.

Hotspur. Cousin, I think thou art enamoured　　　　70
　On his follies: never did I hear
　Of any prince so wild a liberty.
　But be he as he will, yet once ere night
　I will embrace him with a soldier's arm,
　That he shall shrink under my courtesy.
　Arm, arm with speed, and, fellows, soldiers, friends,
　Better consider what you have to do
　Than I, that have not well the gift of tongue,
　Can lift your blood up with persuasion.

Enter a Messenger

Messenger. My lord, here are letters for you.　　　　80
Hotspur. I cannot read them now;
　O gentlemen, the time of life is short,
　To spend that shortness basely were too long,
　If life did ride upon a dial's point,
　Still ending at the arrival of an hour;

An if we live, we live to tread on kings,
If die, brave death, when princes die with us!
Now, for our consciences, the arms are fair,
When the intent of bearing them is just.

Enter another Messenger

Messenger. My lord, prepare, the king comes on apace.   90
Hotspur. I thank him that he cuts me from my tale,
  For I profess not talking; only this—
  Let each man do his best: and here draw I
  A sword, whose temper I intend to stain
  With the best blood that I can meet withal
  In the adventure of this perilous day.
  Now, Esperance! Percy! and set on!
  Sound all the lofty instruments of war,
  And by that music let us all embrace,
  For, heaven to earth, some of us never shall   100
  A second time do such a courtesy.
       The trumpets sound. They embrace, and exeunt

SCENES III, IV, AND V

Plain between the camps

*The King enters with his power. Alarum to the battle. Then
       enter Douglas and Sir Walter Blunt*

Blunt. What is thy name, that in the battle thus
  Thou crossest me? what honour dost thou seek
  Upon my head?
Douglas.   Know then, my name is Douglas;
  And I do haunt thee in the battle thus,
  Because some tell me that thou art a king.
Blunt. They tell thee true.
Douglas. The Lord of Stafford dear to-day hath bought
  Thy likeness, for instead of thee, King Harry,
  This sword hath ended him: so shall it thee,
  Unless thou yield thee as my prisoner.   10

Blunt. I was not born a yielder, thou proud Scot;
  And thou shalt find a king that will revenge
  Lord Stafford's death.   *They fight. Douglas kills Blunt*

Enter Hotspur

Hotspur. O Douglas, hadst thou fought at Holmedon thus,
  I never had triumph'd upon a Scot.
Douglas. All 's done, all 's won; here breathless lies the king.
Hotspur. Where?
Douglas. Here.
Hotspur. This, Douglas? no: I know this face full well:
  A gallant knight he was, his name was Blunt,   20
  Semblably furnish'd like the king himself.
Douglas. A fool go with thy soul, whither it goes!
  A borrow'd title hast thou bought too dear:
  Why didst thou tell me that thou wert a king?
Hotspur. The king hath many marching in his coats.
Douglas. Now, by my sword, I will kill all his coats;
  I'll murder all his wardrobe, piece by piece,
  Until I meet the king.
Hotspur.   Up, and away!
  Our soldiers stand full fairly for the day.   *Exeunt*

Alarum. Enter Falstaff, solus

Falstaff. Though I could 'scape shot-free at London, I   30
fear the shot here, here's no scoring but upon the pate.
Soft, who are you? Sir Walter Blunt, there's honour
for you, here's no vanity; I am as hot as molten lead,
and as heavy too: God keep lead out of me, I need
no more weight than mine own bowels. I have led
my ragamuffins where they are pepper'd, there's not
three of my hundred and fifty left alive, and they are
for the town's end, to beg during life. But who comes
here?

Enter the Prince

Prince. What, stand'st thou idle here? lend me thy sword: 40
Many a noble man lies stark and stiff
Under the hoofs of vaunting enemies,
Whose deaths are yet unreveng'd: I prithee lend me
    thy sword.

Falstaff. O Hal, I prithee give me leave to breathe a
while; Turk Gregory never did such deeds in arms as I
have done this day, I have paid Percy, I have made
him sure.

Prince. He is, indeed; and living to kill thee.
I prithee lend me thy sword.

Falstaff. Nay, before God, Hal, if Percy be alive, thou   50
get'st not my sword, but take my pistol, if thou wilt.

Prince. Give it me: what, is it in the case?

Falstaff. Ay, Hal, 'tis hot, 'tis hot, there's that will sack a
city.

The Prince draws it out, and finds it to be a bottle of sack

Prince. What, is it a time to jest and dally now?
                    He throws the bottle at him. Exit

Falstaff. Well, if Percy be alive, I'll pierce him. If he do
come in my way, so; if he do not, if I come in his
willingly, let him make a carbonado of me. I like not
such grinning honour as Sir Walter hath, give me life,
which if I can save, so; if not, honour comes unlook'd   60
for, and there's an end.   *Exit*

*Alarum. Excursions. Enter the King, the Prince, Lord John of
Lancaster, and Earl of Westmoreland*

King. I prithee,
Harry, withdraw thyself; thou bleed'st too much.
Lord John of Lancaster, go you with him.

85

Lancaster. Not I, my lord, unless I did bleed too.
Prince. I beseech your majesty, make up,
  Lest your retirement do amaze your friends.
King. I will do so.
  My Lord of Westmoreland, lead him to his tent.
Westmoreland. Come, my lord, I'll lead you to your tent.
Prince. Lead me, my lord? I do not need your help: 10
  And God forbid a shallow scratch should drive
  The Prince of Wales from such a field as this,
  Where stain'd nobility lies trodden on,
  And rebels' arms triumph in massacres!
Lancaster. We breathe too long, come, cousin Westmore-
    land,
  Our duty this way lies; for God's sake, come.
                    Exeunt Prince John and Westmoreland
Prince. By God, thou hast deceiv'd me, Lancaster,
  I did not think thee lord of such a spirit;
  Before, I loved thee as a brother, John,
  But now, I do respect thee as my soul.   20
King. I saw him hold Lord Percy at the point,
  With lustier maintenance than I did look for
  Of such an ungrown warrior.
Prince.   O, this boy
  Lends mettle to us all!   *Exit*

                  Enter Douglas

Douglas. Another king? they grow like Hydra's heads:
  I am the Douglas, fatal to all those
  That wear those colours on them: what art thou,
  That counterfeit'st the person of a king?
King. The king himself, who, Douglas, grieves at heart
  So many of his shadows thou hast met   30
  And not the very king. I have two boys
  Seek Percy and thyself about the field,
  But, seeing thou fall'st on me so luckily,
  I will assay thee, and defend thyself.
Douglas. I fear thou art another counterfeit,

And yet, in faith, thou bear'st thee like a king,
But mine I am sure thou art, whoe'er thou be,
And thus I win thee.

They fight; the King being in danger,
re-enter Prince of Wales

Prince. Hold up thy head, vile Scot, or thou art like
  Never to hold it up again! the spirits   40
  Of valiant Shirley, Stafford, Blunt, are in my arms,
  It is the Prince of Wales that threatens thee,
  Who never promiseth but he means to pay.

They fight: Douglas flies

  Cheerly, my lord, how fares your grace?
  Sir Nicholas Gawsey hath for succour sent,
  And so hath Clifton; I'll to Clifton straight.
King. Stay, and breathe awhile:
  Thou hast redeem'd thy lost opinion,
  And show'd thou mak'st some tender of my life,
  In this fair rescue thou hast brought to me.   50
Prince. O God, they did me too much injury
  That ever said I hearken'd for your death;
  If it were so, I might have let alone
  The insulting hand of Douglas over you,
  Which would have been as speedy in your end
  As all the poisonous potions in the world,
  And saved the treacherous labour of your son.
King. Make up to Clifton: I'll to Sir Nicholas Gawsey.

Exit

Enter Hotspur

Hotspur. If I mistake not, thou art Harry Monmouth.
Prince. Thou speak'st as if I would deny my name.   60
Hotspur. My name is Harry Percy.
Prince.   Why, then I see
  A very valiant rebel of the name;
  I am the Prince of Wales, and think not, Percy,
  To share with me in glory any more:
  Two stars keep not their motion in one sphere,

Nor can one England brook a double reign,
Of Harry Percy and the Prince of Wales.
Hotspur. Nor shall it, Harry, for the hour is come
  To end the one of us, and would to God
  Thy name in arms were now as great as mine!   70
Prince. I'll make it greater ere I part from thee,
  And all the budding honours on thy crest
  I'll crop to make a garland for my head.
Hotspur. I can no longer brook thy vanities.   *They fight*

Enter Falstaff

Falstaff. Well said, Hal! to it, Hal! Nay, you shall find no
  boy's play here, I can tell you.

*Re-enter Douglas; he fights with Falstaff, who falls down as
if he were dead, and exit Douglas. Hotspur is wounded, and
falls*

Hotspur. O, Harry, thou hast robb'd me of my youth;
  I better brook the loss of brittle life
  Than those proud titles thou hast won of me;
  They wound my thoughts worse than thy sword my
    flesh,   80
  But thoughts the slaves of life, and life time's fool,   †
  And time, that takes survey of all the world,
  Must have a stop. O, I could prophesy,
  But that the earthy and cold hand of death
  Lies on my tongue: no, Percy, thou art dust,
  And food for—   *Dies*
Prince. For worms, brave Percy: fare thee well, great
  heart!
  Ill-weav'd ambition, how much art thou shrunk!
  When that this body did contain a spirit,
  A kingdom for it was too small a bound,   90
  But now two paces of the vilest earth
  Is room enough: this earth that bears thee dead
  Bears not alive so stout a gentleman;
  If thou wert sensible of courtesy,

I should not make so dear a show of zeal,
But let my favours hide thy mangled face,
And, even in thy behalf, I'll thank myself
For doing these fair rites of tenderness;
Adieu, and take thy praise with thee to heaven,
Thy ignominy sleep with thee in the grave,   100
But not remember'd in thy epitaph!

He spieth Falstaff on the ground

What, old acquaintance, could not all this flesh
Keep in a little life? Poor Jack, farewell;
I could have better spar'd a better man:
O, I should have a heavy miss of thee,
If I were much in love with vanity!
Death hath not struck so fat a deer to-day,
Though many dearer, in this bloody fray.
Embowell'd will I see thee by and by:
Till then in blood by noble Percy lie.   *Exit*   110

Falstaff. (*rising up*) Embowelled? if thou embowel me
to-day, I'll give you leave to powder me and eat me
too to-morrow. 'Sblood, 'twas time to counterfeit, or
that hot termagant Scot had paid me scot and lot too.
Counterfeit? I lie, I am no counterfeit, to die is to be a
counterfeit, for he is but the counterfeit of a man who
hath not the life of a man: but to counterfeit dying
when a man thereby liveth, is to be no counterfeit, but
the true and perfect image of life indeed. The better
part of valour is discretion, in the which better part I   120
have saved my life. 'Zounds, I am afraid of this gun-
powder Percy, though he be dead, how if he should
counterfeit too and rise? by my faith, I am afraid he
would prove the better counterfeit, therefore I'll make
him sure, yea, and I'll swear I kill'd him. Why may he
not rise as well as I? Nothing confutes me but eyes,
and nobody sees me. Therefore, sirrah (*stabbing him*),
with a new wound in your thigh, come you along with
me.   *Takes up Hotspur on his back*

89

Re-enter the Prince of Wales and Lord John of Lancaster

Prince. Come, brother John; full bravely hast thou flesh'd 130
    Thy maiden sword.
Lancaster.   But, soft! whom have we here?
    Did you not tell me this fat man was dead?
Prince. I did, I saw him dead,
    Breathless and bleeding on the ground. Art thou alive?
    Or is it fantasy that plays upon our eyesight?
    I prithee speak, we will not trust our eyes
    Without our ears, thou art not what thou seem'st.
Falstaff. No, that's certain, I am not a double man: but if
    I be not Jack Falstaff, then am I a Jack. There is Percy
    (*throwing the body down*): if your father will do me 140
    any honour, so; if not, let him kill the next Percy him-
    self. I look to be either earl or duke, I can assure you.
Prince. Why, Percy I kill'd myself, and saw thee dead.
Falstaff. Didst thou? Lord, Lord, how this world is given
    to lying! I grant you I was down, and out of breath,
    and so was he, but we rose both at an instant, and
    fought a long hour by Shrewsbury clock; if I may be
    believ'd, so; if not, let them that should reward valour
    bear the sin upon their own heads. I'll take it upon my
    death, I gave him this wound in the thigh: if the man 150
    were alive, and would deny it, 'zounds, I would make
    him eat a piece of my sword.
Lancaster. This is the strangest tale that ever I heard.
Prince. This is the strangest fellow, brother John.
    Come, bring your luggage nobly on your back:
    For my part, if a lie may do thee grace,
    I'll gild it with the happiest terms I have.
                        A retreat is sounded
    The trumpet sounds retreat, the day is ours.
    Come, brother, let us to the highest of the field,
    To see what friends are living, who are dead. 160
               Exeunt Prince of Wales and Lancaster

Falstaff. I'll follow, as they say, for reward. He that re-
wards me, God reward him! If I do grow great, I'll
grow less, for I'll purge, and leave sack, and live
cleanly as a nobleman should do.   *Exit*

*The trumpets sound. Enter the King, Prince of Wales, Lord
John of Lancaster, Earl of Westmoreland, with Worcester and
Vernon prisoners*

King. Thus ever did rebellion find rebuke.
　　Ill-spirited Worcester, did not we send grace,
　　Pardon, and terms of love to all of you?
　　And wouldst thou turn our offers contrary?
　　Misuse the tenour of thy kinsman's trust?
　　Three knights upon our party slain to-day,
　　A noble earl and many a creature else,
　　Had been alive this hour,
　　If like a Christian thou hadst truly borne
　　Betwixt our armies true intelligence.   10
Worcester. What I have done my safety urg'd me to;
　　And I embrace this fortune patiently,
　　Since not to be avoided it falls on me.
King. Bear Worcester to the death, and Vernon too:
　　Other offenders we will pause upon.
　　　　　　　Exeunt Worcester and Vernon, guarded
　　How goes the field?
Prince. The noble Scot, Lord Douglas, when he saw
　　The fortune of the day quite turn'd from him,
　　The noble Percy slain, and all his men
　　Upon the foot of fear, fled with the rest,   20
　　And falling from a hill, he was so bruis'd
　　That the pursuers took him. At my tent
　　The Douglas is; and I beseech your grace
　　I may dispose of him.

91

King.   With all my heart.

Prince. Then, brother John of Lancaster, to you
 This honourable bounty shall belong:
 Go to the Douglas, and deliver him
 Up to his pleasure, ransomless and free:
 His valour shown upon our crests to-day
 Hath taught us how to cherish such high deeds   30
 Even in the bosom of our adversaries.

Lancaster. I thank your grace for this high courtesy,
 Which I shall give away immediately.

King. Then this remains, that we divide our power.
 You, son John, and my cousin Westmoreland
 Towards York shall bend you with your dearest speed,
 To meet Northumberland and the prelate Scroop,
 Who, as we hear, are busily in arms:
 Myself and you, son Harry, will towards Wales,
 To fight with Glendower and the Earl of March.   40
 Rebellion in this land shall lose his sway,
 Meeting the check of such another day,
 And since this business so fair is done,
 Let us not leave till all our own be won.   *Exeunt*

Notes

I. i. 5. *entrance*; though the general sense is clear, it cannot be pretended that this, though read by both Q and F, is as clear as one could wish; but the emendations, such as *entrails*, *entrants*, or *Erinnys*, are not much better.

I. i. 30. *Therefore we meet not now*; i.e. 'that is not what we are now meeting about.'

I. ii. 110. *Sir John Sack, and Sugar Jack? how . . .* ; so Q. Usually repunctuated to read *Sir John Sack and Sugar? Jack, how . . .* , perhaps rightly, but not, I think, essentially.

I. iii. 6. *than my condition*; i.e. 'I will be the *king* that I am rather than the much milder *man* that by natural disposition I am.'

II. i. 35. *Nay, by God, soft*; Q reads *Nay by God soft*, and though the expurgator of F clearly took it in the sense given by the usual punctuation, since F reads *soft I pray ye*, I suspect that an expletive of the 'God's sonties' type is concealed.

II. i. 75. *tranquillity . . . oneyers*; I can see no reason for the spate of conjectural emendations: Gadshill is deliberately playing with and coining words. (But it should perhaps be noticed that Q reads *oneyres*.)

II. iii. 30-31. *divide myself and go to buffets*; i.e. 'come to blows with myself.'

II. iv. 115. *pitiful-hearted butter*; Theobald's emendation of Q and F, *pitiful-hearted Titan*. Easier still, perhaps, would be simply to omit the second *Titan* (assuming perhaps that *Titan* was an interlinear correction of *the sun*, which found its way into the wrong place as well as the right).

II. iv. 390. *so youth*; so Q. The F reading, *yet youth*, is usually accepted; but I see no reason to suppose that Falstaff in adopting Euphuistic diction will be too careful of sense.

II. iv. 432. *Swearest thou, ungracious boy?*; an amusing instance of the expurgator. F in Falstaff's speech tones down

'Sblood to I'faith (and omits i' faith altogether), so making the Prince's remark quite pointless.

II. iv. 479. *made*; thus both Q and F. Most editions read *mad*, which seems to make the fog of an obscure—and very probably corrupt—passage denser than before.

II. iv. 532–33. *his death will be a march of twelve-score*; twelve-score yards was the length of an archery range; this is explained as meaning that twelve-score yards afoot will be the death of Falstaff.

III. i. 54. *Why I can teach you . . .* ; the omission of the un-essential *cousin* will cure the metre.

III. i. 195. *She is . . .* ; this speech of Glendower's, in the middle of a steady run of verse, is a good example of the verse corrupted into prose, or prose only halfway towards becoming verse, which we meet in this play (see note on III. iii. 194).

III. iii. 57. *tithe*; Theobald's emendation for the *right* of Q (cf. III. i. 137).

III. iii. 194. *Go bear . . . afternoon*; this is a good instance of the many passages in the play which sound as if they were, so to speak, trying to be verse. There seems no reason why the Prince should begin in prose and then burst into blank verse. If we attach the second *go* to the direction to Bardolph, where it more properly belongs, we have:—

> Peto, to horse, to horse, for thou and I
> Have thirty miles to ride (yet) ere dinner time.
> Jack, meet me to-morrow in the Temple hall
> At two o'clock in the afternoon.

And we can do something with the opening, thus:—

> Go bear this letter to my brother John;
> This to my Lord of Westmoreland. Go

IV. i. 17. *'Zounds . . .* ; and this is an equally good instance of the troubles that attended the process of bowdlerising the

Quarto for the Folio. The Folio 'cutter' omits 'Zounds, and finds himself a syllable short, with *how has he the leisure to be sick*; so he adds a syllable, without regard to scansion, and produces the remarkable 'line' that stands in F:—

> *How has he the leisure to be sick now.*

IV. i. 98. *All plum'd . . .* ; a vexatious passage. Steevens and Malone thought that an entire line had dropped out after *wind*. But if the passage is more or less correct as it stands there can hardly be a doubt, from the staccato line-upon-line rhythm, that we want only one line for each parallel, and that Rowe was on the right track in wanting to find the corruption in *with*, which he thought concealed a verb, such as *wing*. Another possibility, however, is that the *estridges* were a first thought, rejected but inadequately cancelled, and that we should in fact read:—

> *All plum'd like eagles having lately bath'd.*

IV. ii. 3. *Cop-hill*; this is commonly read as Sutton Co'fil (*i.e.* Sutton Coldfield) which is much more satisfactory geographically than graphically. The *Sutton cop-hill* of Q and *Sutton-cop-hill* of F are obstinate, and the hyphen seems to forbid the supposition of an auditory error.

IV. ii. 41. *not a shirt and a half*; Cowl and Morgan excellently compare II. iv. 123 and V. iii. 36 in defending the Q F *not* against the emendatory assaults of editors who wish to read *but* and teach Falstaff logic.

IV. iii. 2. *then*; i.e. 'if you wait.' (The retort is to Worcester not to Hotspur).

IV. iii. 12. *As you . . .* ; we should probably omit either *my lord* or *this day*.

V. iv. 81. *thoughts the slaves of life . . .* ; so Q, which I see no reason to desert for the usual *thought's the slave of life*: in Q *thoughts*, *life*, and *time* are all subjects of *must stop*.

Glossary

MANY words and phrases in Shakespeare require glossing, not because they are in themselves unfamiliar, but for the opposite reason, that Shakespeare uses in their Elizabethan and unfamiliar sense a large number of words which seem so familiar that there is no incentive to look for them in the glossary. It is hoped that a glossary arranged as below will make it easy to see at a glance what words and phrases in any particular scene require elucidation. A number of phrases are glossed by what seems to be, in their context, the modern equivalent rather than by lexicographical glosses on the words which compose them.

Act First

SCENE I

line

2 PANT, recover breath
13 CLOSE, clash
14 MUTUAL, conjoined
18 HIS, its
21 IMPRESSED, pressed for service (*cf. 'pressgang'*)
30 THEREFORE WE MEET NOT NOW, that is not the cause of our present meeting
33 DEAR EXPEDIENCE, 'pet project' (needing haste)

line

35 LIMITS OF THE CHARGE, "definitions of the scope of the enterprise" (Wright)
37 POST, messenger
52 HOLY-ROOD DAY, Holy Cross day (Sept. 14)
54 APPROVED, well-tried
69 BALK'D, (?) heaped up
83 MINION, favourite
98 PRUNE, preen (of a hawk)

SCENE II

2 SACK, white wine from Spain
7 CAPONS, chickens
9 LEAPING-HOUSES, brothels
14 SEVEN STARS, Pleiades (*or* (?) Great Bear)
22 ROUNDLY, plainly
41 HYBLA, mountain of Greece famous for honey

42 DURANCE, (*a*) stout material, (*b*) imprisonment
44 QUIDDITIES, quibbles (*quidditas*)
58 FOBB'D, cheated
59 ANTIC, buffoon
67 JUMPS, suits
70, 71 SUITS, (*a*) petitions, (*b*) clothes

96

Act I Sc. i—*continued*

line
73 GIB, tom
LUGG'D, baited
99 BAFFLE, deride
104 SET A MATCH, plot a robbery (*thieves' slang*)
123 VIZARDS, masks
152–53 ALL-HALLOWN SUMMER, 'Indian summer' (*about All Saints' Day*)

line
172 CASES OF BUCKRAM, overalls of coarse canvas
173 NOTED, well-known
180 WARDS, parries
182 REPROOF, exposure
188 UNYOK'D, unchecked
203 HOPES, expectations
204 SULLEN GROUND, dull background

SCENE III

13 HOLP, helped
PORTLY, dignified
19 FRONTIER, (?) barrier (*or possibly just* 'façade')
27 MISPRISION, misunderstanding
36 MILLINER, dealer in perfumed goods (*orig. from Milan*)
38 POUNCET-BOX, perfume-box
41 TOOK IT IN SNUFF, (*a*) snuffed it, (*b*) took it amiss
50 POPINJAY, coxcomb, an 'Osric'
58 PARMACETI, spermaceti
66 INDIRECTLY, without thinking
77 YET, still
87 INDENT, make an agreement with

97 MOUTHED, gaping
106 CRISP, curled (*i.e. ripples*)
108 POLICY, scheming
113 BELIE, tell (favourable) lies about
137 CANKER'D, malignant
168 PREDICAMENT, category
169 RANGE, stand in ranks
173 GAGE, engage
189 QUICK-CONCEIVING, quickly-comprehending
209 APPREHENDS A WORLD OF FIGURES, moves in a world of fancies
228 DEFY, abjure
240 PISMIRES, ants
241 POLITICIAN, schemer
255 COZENERS, tricksters (*with play on 'cousin'*)
271 BRISTOWE, Bristol

Act Second

SCENE I

6 FLOCKS, tufts of wool (*cf. 'flock mattress'*)
7 OUT OF ALL CESS, immoderately

8 AS A DOG, *meaning uncertain* ('as meaningless as most alliterative similes')
9 BOTS, worms

Act II Sc. i—*continued*

line

14 TENCH, a fish (*liable to parasites*)

20 LOACH, a fish (*also liable to parasites*)

23 GAMMON, leg

23 RAZES, roots (*radices*)

45 CHARGE, baggage

53 FRANKLIN, yeoman

60–61 SAINT NICHOLAS' CLERKS, slang *for* robbers

68 TROJANS, boon-companions

72 LAND-RAKERS, footpads

73 LONG-STAFF SIXPENNY STRIKERS, pickpockets with long staves

86 FERN-SEED, the traditional medicine for invisibility

SCENE II

2 FRETS, (*a*) chafes, (*b*) frays

GUMM'D, stiffened with gum

12 SQUIRE, rule

36 COLT, cheat

48 SETTER, decoy

73 HAPPY MAN BE HIS DOLE, 'good luck, all!'

84 GORBELLIED, fat-bellied

85 CHUFFS, rich rustics

87 GRANDJURORS (*only men of substance could serve on grandjury*)

102 OFFICER, constable

SCENE III

11–12 UNSORTED, unsuitable

14 HIND, boor

47 MANAGE, training of horse

50 FRONTIERS, barricades

51 BASILISKS, largest type of cannon

CULVERIN, smaller cannon

58 MOTIONS, expressions

69 O ESPERANCE, the Percy war-cry

76 SPLEEN, impetuosity

77 TOSS'D, carried this way and that

81 LINE, support (*met. from lining a garment*)

84 DIRECTLY, straightforwardly

90 MAMMETS, dolls

TILT, joust

91 CRACK'D CROWNS, pun on (*a*) broken heads, (*b*) cracked (and so not current) coins

SCENE IV

4 LOGGERHEADS, dolts

5–6 BASE-STRING, lowest string in stringed instrument

6 LEASH, trio

11 CORINTHIAN, 'gay dog'

23 UNDER-SKINKER, barman

26 BASTARD, sweet Spanish wine like muscatel

26–27 'HALF-MOON,' name of the room in the tavern

29 PUNY, novice (*puisne*)

32 PRECEDENT, object-lesson

36 POMGARNET, name of a room (*as 'half-moon' above*)

46 INDENTURE, agreement

Act II   Sc. iv—*continued*

line

68 NOT-PATED, crop-headed
   PUKE, dark-grey
   CADDIS-GARTER, garter of worsted yarn
71 BASTARD, *see* l. 26
89 HUMOURS, moods
111 NETHER STOCKS, stockings
122 SHOTTEN, that has 'shot' its roe
130 DAGGER OF LATH, property dagger (*of the Vice in morality plays*)
187 WARD, guard
205 POINTS, tagged laces fastening hose to doublet
213 KENDAL GREEN, green woollen cloth made at Kendal
219 TALLOW-CATCH, *either* tub, *or* lump, of tallow
228 STRAPPADO, a form of torture
237 NEAT, OX
   STOCK-FISH, dried fish
239 STANDING-TUCK, narrow sword set upright
247 OUT-FAC'D, scared
254 STARTING-HOLE, 'hidy-hole,' *and so* subterfuge
279 AS MUCH . . . ROYAL MAN, *i.e.* a crown

line

304 WITH THE MANNER, in the act
316 BOMBAST, padding
325 AMAMON, one of the devils
327 HOOK, weapon shaped like a billhook (*which in fact had no 'cross' or cross-hilt*)
346 BLUE-CAPS, Scots ('blue-bonnets')
375 CAMBYSES, the traditional ranting tyrant (*from Preston's play,* 1570)
376 LEG, bow
386 TICKLE-BRAIN, strong liquor
397 MICHER, truant
424 RABBIT-SUCKER, sucking rabbit
   POULTER, poulterer
437 BOLTING-HUTCH, flour-bin (*into which the flour is 'bolted,' i.e. sifted*)
438 BOMBARD, large leather jug for liquor
440 VICE, the 'Vice' from the morality plays
512 PAUL'S, *i.e.* St. Paul's
534 ADVANTAGE, interest

Act Third

SCENE I

2 INDUCTION, preliminaries
14 CRESSETS, beacons
30 BELDAM, grandmother
47 HOLD ME PACE, keep up with me
71 HITHERTO, to this point
77 INDENTURES, agreements

95 CRANKING, twisting
97 CANTLE, piece
102 BOTTOM, valley
107 GELDING, diminishing
112 CHARGE, expense
128 CANSTICK, candlestick
   TURN'D, *i.e. on the lathe*

Act III   Sc. i—*continued*

line

146 MOLDWARP, mole
160 CATES, delicacies
161 SUMMER-HOUSE, summer
  residence in country
169 HUMOUR, mood
171 TEMPTED, provoked
182 OPINION (*i.e. of oneself*),
  arrogance
189 SPITE, vexation
196 HARLOTRY, 'baggage'
205 HIGHLY, in elevated style
207 DIVISION, variation
229 HUMOROUS, moody
234 BRACH, bitch
246 COMFIT-MAKER, confec-
  tioner

line

249 SARCENET, thin taffeta (*i.e.
  'you swear like a draper's
  wife'*)
253 PEPPER-GINGERBREAD,
  coarse gingerbread
254 VELVET-GUARDS, *lit.* velvet
  trimmings (*the whole
  line means 'Citizens and
  their wives in their Sun-
  day best'*)
257–58 REDBREAST   TEACHER,
  trainer of singing birds
262 BOOK IS DRAWN, agreement
  is drawn up

SCENE II

line

13 LEWD, ignorant
20 DOUBTLESS, confident
25 PICK-THANKS, flatterers
61 BAVIN, brushwood faggots
  (soon burnt out)
62 CARDED, debase by mixing
  (*met. from mixing
  liquors*)
67 COMPARATIVE, rival, companion
69 ENFEOFF'D, surrendered
77 COMMUNITY, the common-
  ness of the sight

line

82 IN HIS FACE, in his presence
83 CLOUDY, sullen
109 MAJORITY, pre-eminence
115 ENLARGED, freed
120 CAPITULATE, conspire
125 START OF SPLEEN, sudden
  impulse
147 FACTOR, agent
148 ENGROSS, 'corner'
157 BANDS, bonds
159 PARCEL, piece
167 HEAD, body of troops

SCENE III

2 BATE, pine
4 APPLE-JOHN, a shrivelled
  apple
8 PEPPERCORN, *as being small
  and shrivelled*
9 BREWER'S HORSE, *as tradi-
  tionally broken down*
10 SPOIL, ruin

25 ADMIRAL, chief ship
39 BALL OF WILDFIRE, firework
42 LINKS, torches
46 SALAMANDER, a creature
  supposed to live in fire
52 DAME PARTLET, traditional
  name for the wife of
  Chanticleer

Act III Sc. iii—*continued*

line

69 DOWLAS, coarse linen
70 BOLTERS, cloths for sifting meal
71 HOLLAND, fine lawn
73 BY-DRINKING, drinks between meals
79 DENIER, a coin of trifling value
79–80 MAKE A YOUNKER OF ME, treat me as a boy
85 SNEAK-CUP, *either* (*a*) one who shirks his liquor, *or* (*b*) a cup-thief

line

112 STEW'D PRUNE, traditional dish of prostitutes
113 DRAWN FOX, *either* (*a*) fox drawn from cover (and so using all his tricks), *or* (*b*) a 'drag' fox
114 MAID MARIAN, a hoydenish character in morris dancing
115 TO, as compared to
134 OUGHT, owed
156–57 EMBOSS'D, swollen
201 FURNITURE, equipment

Act Fourth

SCENE I

9 APPROVE, test
34 DEAR, critical
37 CONJUNCTION, joint force
47 MAIN, stake
51 LIST, boundary
56 COMFORT OF RETIREMENT LIVES IN THIS, this gives us the possibility of secure retreat
61 HAIR, texture, *and so*, character

69 OFFERING, challenging
71 LOOP, loophole
96 DAFF'D ASIDE, gave the go-by to
98 ESTRIDGES, goshawks
99 BAITED, fluttered
105 CUISSES, thigh-pieces
118 REPRISAL, prize
126 DRAW, mobilise

SCENE II

6 MAKES, amounts to
11 SOUS'D GURNET, pickled gurnard
12 PRESS, commission to impress
19 CALIVER, arquebus
23 ANCIENTS, ensigns

25 PAINTED CLOTH, painted canvas (*as cheap substitute for arras*)
29 TRADE-FALLEN, out-of-work
OF, produced by
35 DRAFF, pig-wash
40 GYVES, fetters
48 BLOWN, swollen
64 TOSS, *sc. on pikes*

SCENE III

line | line
26 BATED, exhausted
62 SUE HIS LIVERY, ask for the delivery to him of his lands (*a legal phrase*)

68 CAP AND KNEE, hats off and bowing
88 PERSONAL, in person
92 IN THE NECK OF, 'on the head of'

SCENE IV

10 TOUCH, test
17 RATED SINEW, valued support

25 HEAD, band
31 MOE, more (*Eliz. plur.*)

Act Fifth

SCENE I

2 BUSKY, bushy
17 ORB, orbit
24 ENTERTAIN, occupy
29 CHEWET, chough (*a chattering bird*)
51 SUFFERANCES, suffering
57 GRIPE, grasp
60 GULL, unfledged bird
66 HEAD, power
77 RUB THE ELBOW, *i.e.* as an expression of satisfaction

('*rub their hands*')
88 SET OFF HIS HEAD, being removed from the account
111 WAIT ON US, are our ministers
123 COLOSSUS, enormous statue bestriding the harbour at Rhodes
139 SCUTCHEON, funeral hatchment

SCENE II

62 CITAL, recital

84 DIAL'S POINT, clock-hand

SCENE III

21 SEMBLABLY, similarly
30 SHOT-FREE, without paying
31 SCORING, (*a*) entering an account, (*b*) slashing

45 TURK GREGORY, Pope Gregory VII (supposed 'cruel as a Turk')
58 CARBONADO, meat slashed and broiled

SCENE IV

5 MAKE UP, go to the front
15 BREATHE, 'take a breather'
25 HYDRA, the serpent which

grew two fresh heads for each that Hercules cut off

GLOSSARY

Act V Sc. iv—*continued*

line

49 TENDER, regard for
94 SENSIBLE, sensitive to
95 DEAR, truly felt
96 FAVOUR, scarf or glove worn
    in helmet
105 MISS, loss

line

109 EMBOWELL'D, disembow-
    elled (as of a deer, but
    here with suggestion of
    embalmment)
114 TERMAGANT, furious
    SCOT AND LOT, in full

L2